HOW TO PARTNER WITH GIRL SCOUT AMBASSADORS ON JUSTICE

IT'S YOUR PLANET—LOVE IT! A LEADERSHIP JOURNEY

A Girl Scout leadership journey invites girls to explore a [illegible]
through many experiences and from many perspectives.
All the joys of travel are built right in: meeting new people, exploring new things,
making memories, gathering keepsakes. This guide is your suitcase.
It's packed with everything you need for a wonderful trip that will change girls' lives.

Girl Scouts of the USA

Girl Scouts®

WRITTEN BY David Bjerklie and Valerie Takahama

ILLUSTRATED BY Toi James, Andrea Bastiani Archibald, Kate Gottlieb, Kathleen Sweeney

DESIGNED BY Alexander Isley Inc.

EXECUTIVE EDITOR, JOURNEYS: Laura Tuchman

MANAGER, OPERATIONS: Sharon Kaplan

MANAGER, PROGRAM DESIGN: Sarah Micklem

First published in 2009 by Girl Scouts of the USA
420 Fifth Avenue, New York, NY 10018-2798
www.girlscouts.org

ISBN: 978-0-88441-742-2

Printed in Italy

1 2 3 4 5 6 7 8 9/17 16 15 14 13 12 11 10 09

Text printed on Fredrigoni Cento 40 percent de-inked, post-consumer fibers and 60 percent secondary recycled fibers.

Covers printed on Prisma artboard FSC Certified mixed sources.

Mixed Sources
Product group from well-managed forests and other controlled sources
www.fsc.org Cert no. SQS-COC-100209
© 1996 Forest Stewardship Council
FSC

CONTENTS

“Most people put the environment and the economy in opposite camps. But you can’t achieve environmental integrity . . . without . . . social and economic justice.”

—Gwendolyn Hallsmith, director of planning and community development for Montpelier, Vermont

David McNew/Getty Images News/Getty Images

The Challenge of Justice

Justice.

You've probably wished for it, for Earth and all its inhabitants, at some point in your life.

Ambassadors long for it, too. This journey is their opportunity—and yours!—to SOAR toward the lofty ideals of justice. As the girls (and you) embark on a search for a meaningful and workable equation for justice, they'll investigate some hard realities. Then they'll set their idealism free as they explore what justice asks of each and every one of us.

Much of what girls do in Girls Scouts (and in their busy lives) is, well, do, do, do! As you and the girls begin the search for justice, you'll find it useful to keep in mind that while plenty of "do-ing" is possible, this is, at its heart, a journey about thinking and believing.

Who needs justice most? Why is it so difficult to attain? Why is it worth the struggle?

If girls don't get time to find their own answers to questions related to justice, they won't be motivated to create more of it on Earth!

JUSTICE starts with the belief that it *is* possible. As you guide the girls toward a new equation for justice, you are continuing an enduring tradition. An appreciation for the natural world and the need to care for Planet Earth have been at the core of Girl Scouting since its founding in 1912. As ***JUSTICE*** makes clear, doing right by the planet means doing right by people, too. So . . . journey forward!

Journey to *JUSTICE*

YOU'RE ON THIS JOURNEY, TOO!

As you prepare to guide Ambassadors on this journey, it may be helpful to pause and consider your own ideas about justice. What ideas and images come to mind when you hear the word *justice*? Laws and courts, robes and gavels? Maybe you also think of the scales of justice, or the saying "justice is blind."

What thoughts and personal experiences can you share with the girls about the struggle for fairness? In what context have you heard of environmental justice?

In their book, Ambassadors will read about the historic examples of Warren County, North Carolina, and Love Canal in New York. Can you think of similar examples that you are familiar with? Don't worry: If you haven't yet, you soon will. No experience is needed on this journey to *JUSTICE*.

On this journey, the challenge of identifying environmental injustices, understanding how they arise, and realizing how solutions to them can be found are opportunities for Ambassadors to develop valuable leadership skills they can use now and throughout their lives. Plus, they'll be networking—with scientists, community leaders, environmentalists, and others, all of whom can offer valuable advice about college, careers, and other aspects of life after high school.

JUSTICE goes beyond simple matters of right and wrong. Justice is about fairness, understanding, and compassion—and how present circumstances must be understood in terms of both the past and the future. Above all, environmental justice is a powerful perspective, a way of seeing issues and people, and solutions to environmental problems.

Throughout *JUSTICE*, girls will encounter case studies of environmental injustices and consider the circumstances and decisions that led to them—and to efforts to remedy them. In many cases, health will be the most obvious measure of environmental justice. A community's health and well-being depend on a range of factors that affect people where they live, work, learn, and play. Our quality of life depends on the quality of our environment.

In this way, the journey engages girls in developing into leaders who understand the need to strive for environmental justice, and who can also move forward to make a difference in any arena they choose.

HEARTS AND MINDS

So much information is now available about environmental problems facing our planet and what must be done to correct them. *JUSTICE* is part of a series of Girl Scout leadership journeys that invites girls, and their families and adult volunteers, to make sense of that information so they can act for the betterment of Earth.

The umbrella theme for the series—*It's Your Planet—Love It!*—came directly from a brainstorm with teen Girl Scouts. Its sentiment is clear: The desire to nurture and protect is first and foremost an act of love. If girls love Planet Earth and all its wonders, they will naturally be moved to protect it. Love for Planet Earth is the true and necessary starting point for thoughtful and sustained environmental action.

You may already be deeply committed to environmental causes—or not. Either way, you will be guiding girls on a journey of learning and doing that benefits them and the world.

ENCOURAGING SCIENTIFIC MINDS

All along, *JUSTICE* engages girls in science, math, the outdoors, and environmental stewardship. You may be an expert in one or all of these areas—or none. No matter—there's no need to have all the answers! All you need to guide your group of Ambassadors is right here in this book. Just add your own sense of wonder, and an eagerness to explore all that justice can offer and accomplish.

Imagine the power of more than 60,000 Ambassadors and their volunteers and families making choices that improve and protect Earth's resources. What are you waiting for? Start striving for *JUSTICE*!

Toward the Sage Award, and Interviewing Tips

AS YOU REVIEW THE AWARD STEPS, THINK ABOUT:

- Your own life experiences and what they've taught you about speaking up for what you believe in.
- People you know in the community and the connections they may have.
- Strengths, talents, and skills you possess that you can share with the girls.

On this journey to JUSTICE, Ambassadors have the opportunity to earn the prestigious Sage Award by participating in activities in the six steps to understanding environmental justice. The Sage Award takes its name from the word meaning wise person (from the Latin root *sapere*, to be wise) and the medicinal herb (from the Latin root *salvare*, to heal or to save). The award represents both the commitment and ability to be judicious, and it reminds us of the importance of healing.

The 6 Steps to Earning Sage

1 **LOOK HIGH, LOOK WIDE**

2 **DO the MATH**

3 **Be HAWK-EYED**

4 **Take the SCIENTIFIC View**

5 **DECIPHER Decisions**

6 **Write Your Equation and PRESENT It**

Interviewing Tips

Several of the steps toward the Sage Award engage girls in interviewing adults in their community. This is a great opportunity for girls to expand their network, get fresh ideas for educational and career paths, and bring real-life insights to their equations for justice. Suggestions for how to identify people to interview are included in Sessions 5 and 6, along with tips about how to conduct good interviews. Coach the Ambassadors to get the most out of their interviews by offering these general tips, too:

Small Team Interviews Are Best: If the whole Ambassador group interviews one expert, it will be hard for each girl to be fully involved! So try to encourage the team to identify several adults and then divide into small teams to conduct the interviews.

Safety Always Matters: The team may arrange to bring guests to their gatherings to interview them, or they may go on mini-field trips to conduct the interviews. Make sure the Ambassadors do not arrange to meet adults on their own, that interviews take place in public places during business hours, and that the girls are always accompanied by an adult volunteer or parent.

In Person Is Best: Whenever possible, in-person interviews offer more opportunities to have a relaxed and free-flowing conversation. But girls can also interview by phone or e-mail, and these methods allow them to cast a wider net in search of decision-makers.

Do Some Advance Research: Girls may have general questions they want answers for, but the circumstances of every expert are unique. So urge girls to find out as much as they can about the larger context of the work done by the people they are interviewing.

Prepare: That includes having a note pad, two pens, and questions written out. You'll find examples of questions the girls may want to ask in Sessions 5 and 6. These are just ideas; the girls will likely think of many others! Prepare the Ambassadors to be flexible. Interviewers nearly always find that they need to ask questions that didn't initially occur to them during their research. They also find that some of the questions they thought would be quite good actually don't apply or need to be modified.

Be Accurate: That means getting all the answers down correctly. But it also means knowing when you haven't understood an answer or are not sure you got it right. In moments of uncertainty, interviewers must always stop and say, "I'm not sure I understood that. Did you mean . . . ?" Reporters do that every day—without any worries at all of seeming awkward!

STEP BACK AND LET GO

As girls move through the steps to their equation for justice, consider "fading facilitation," a process in which your role decreases as the girls move deeper into their projects. The more they do, the more confident they become—and the less active you are. Your success is actually measured by how much you let go!

Snapshot of the Journey

SESSION 1 Toward Justice	The Ambassadors begin to think about what justice asks of each of us as individuals. They examine the ways in which environmental concerns can be ranked based on various needs and perspectives. They go on to explore how desires for justice compete with self-interests. The girls: • create a list of what matters to them about the environment • consider their plans and goals, and how to best customize the journey
SESSION 2 Look High, Look Wide	The Ambassadors find ways to see the big picture of environmental justice issues. As they explore what it means to "sit at every stone" in search of justice, they also consider how a "high and wide" perspective can help them resolve conflicts in their own relationships. The girls: • see how images can be used to tell many different stories • consider what parts of their equations for justice are starting to take shape
SESSION 3 Do the Math	The Ambassadors identify ways to lighten their step on the planet and make a commitment to follow through and record their results. They explore how Doing the Math can be an effective motivation and communication tool in the quest for environmental justice. The girls: • create a simple survey to explore the environmental concerns of others • create a "guilty habits" list to help them commit to Doing the Math
SESSION 4 Be Hawk-Eyed	The Ambassadors sharpen their critical eye for environmental issues by learning to look beyond the hype. They also consider how getting the facts can be a good strategy for conflict resolution. The girls: • explore how media and advertising persuades viewers • check in on how they are Doing the Math
SESSION 5 Take the Scientific View	The Ambassadors investigate the role of science and uncertainty in environmental justice issues by interviewing scientists. The girls: • explore how "expert" opinions intertwine in environmental justice issues • consider what science can and cannot do for the environment

SESSION 6 **Decipher Decisions**	The Ambassadors explore the complexity of decision-making when various needs compete. Ultimately, they develop ideas about "just decision-making" to add to their growing equations for justice. The girls: • interview decision-makers about the many variables they grapple with • share some of the great decisions they have made in their own lives
SESSION 7 **What's the Equation?**	The Ambassadors access Add It In notes and ideas they've made along the journey, create their definition and equation for justice, and choose the audience for their presentation. They also consider some "new equations" for themselves as they talk about what they have learned about career options along their journey. The girls also: • begin planning their final celebration of the journey
SESSION 8 **Who Will Listen?**	The Ambassadors continue to plan their presentation to define justice and share an equation for achieving it. The girls also: • discuss how aspects of their equations can also help in addressing conflicts in relationships
SESSION 9 **Inspiring Justice**	The Ambassadors share their vision of justice—what it means and how we get it—with others and invite everyone to make strides toward justice by Doing the Math. Following their presentation, girls take time to talk through everything they've explored along the journey. The girls also: • celebrate their experience based on their plans—perhaps even "passing it on" in some way to others
SESSION 10 **Celebrate!**	The Ambassadors reflect on what they have learned along their journey toward justice, enjoy a closing celebration, and take a look at how they might continue their pursuit of justice. The girls also: • celebrate their experience based on their plans—and consider how to keep their equations and their search for justice growing

Health, Safety, and Well-Being

SAFETY FIRST

Keep the Girl Scout reference *Safety-Wise* handy. It details the safety net provided for girls in Girl Scouting. Use it along with any additional information from your council to plan trips and outdoor activities, and to promote the well-being of the Ambassadors every time you get together. It will be particularly useful as the girls explore their communities and enjoy any other group outings.

The emotional and physical safety and well-being of girls is of paramount importance in Girl Scouting. Look out for the safety of girls by following *Safety-Wise* when planning all gatherings and trips, and:

- check into any additional safety guidelines your Girl Scout council might provide, based on local issues
- talk to girls and their families about special needs or concerns

Welcoming Girls with Disabilities

Girl Scouting embraces girls with many different needs and is guided by a very specific and positive philosophy of inclusion that benefits all: Each girl is an equal and valued member of a group with typically developing peers.

As an adult volunteer, you have the chance to improve the way society views girls with disabilities. One way to start is with language. Your words have a huge impact on the process of inclusion. People-First Language puts the person before the disability:

SAY	INSTEAD OF
She has autism.	She's autistic.
She has an intellectual disability.	She's mentally retarded.
She has a learning disability.	The girl is learning-disabled.
She uses a wheelchair.	She is wheelchair-bound.
She has a disability.	She is handicapped.

LEARN WHAT A GIRL NEEDS

First, don't assume that because a person has a disability, she needs assistance or special accommodations. Probably the most important thing you can do is to ask the individual girl or her parents or guardians what she needs to make her experience in Girl Scouts successful. If you are frank with the girl and her parents and make yourself accessible to them, it's likely they will respond in kind, creating a better experience for all.

It's important for all girls to be rewarded based on their best efforts—not on completion of a task. Give any girl the opportunity to do her best and she will. Sometimes that means changing a few rules or approaching an activity in a more creative way. Here are a few examples:

- Invite a girl to perform an activity after observing others doing it first.
- Ask the girls to come up with ideas on how to adapt an activity.
- Often what counts most is staying flexible and varying your approach. For a list of resources, visit www.girlscouts.org and search on "disability resources."

GIRL SCOUT COUNCIL CONTACT INFO

Name: ________________

____

____

Can help with: ________________

____

____

Phone: ________________

E-mail: ________________

Soaring into Math, Science, and Engineering

JUSTICE directly engages girls in understanding that everything on Earth is affected by issues of environmental justice. People, animals, plants, microscopic organisms—everything alive can benefit from justice.

As the Ambassadors learn about the environmental issues all around them, they will also see that science, math, and engineering are as much a part of daily life as issues of justice. Yet a troublesome gap often develops between girls' interest and ability in these subjects and their desire and confidence to pursue higher education, and ultimately careers, in these fields. By eighth grade, only half as many girls as boys in the United States are interested in careers in science, technology, engineering, and math (STEM). Those numbers get even worse in high school and college. Fewer than 1 in 5 of all college engineering degrees are awarded to women. And even among these women, a great many leave the profession in their 30s and 40s. Women are also under-represented in the fields of chemistry and physics.

GUIDE THE AMBASSADORS TO SEEK OUT ROLE MODELS

Tap your own experience and enthusiasm, and the resources of other women in your community. In the process, you will expand your own horizons and appreciation of how science, technology, engineering, and math can be used to make a difference in the world.

BUILDING SCIENTIFIC MINDS

To sustain interest and build confidence, Girl Scouts believes that early exposure to the joys and wonders of these subjects is crucial—as is encouragement from families, teachers, and the media that is so much a part of daily life. What's key is ending the many myths and biases that girls encounter when pursuing these subjects. The other part of the challenge is for girls to realize that science, technology, engineering, and math offer ways to help people and communities. On this journey, Ambassadors have a direct opportunity to experience how essential these subjects are to any desire to protect Planet Earth. This journey aims to foster lifelong interests in those subjects, and in every aspect of justice.

So take advantage of each time STEM subjects pop up in the girls' lives. Sirens in the night? A lesson in decibels. Cell phones beeping? Modern technology as daily distraction. A line of smog or a fresh ocean breeze? A reminder of Earth's atmosphere, and how countries halfway around the world are our next-door neighbors when it comes to air.

As *JUSTICE* makes clear, even time spent in the kitchen involves endless math problems. Cooking combines chemistry and a lot of math—ratios, measurements, proportions. What's a measuring cup, after all, but a basic math tool? A flattened cake pulled from the oven might signal a scientific misfire. Not enough eggs, perhaps? Or no baking powder? And think of breads, cakes, and cookies, and all their exacting needs. Cooks might dispense with measuring tools, but bakers rarely can. Even the most intuitive of them play by the numbers.

Make the most of every creative scientific moment that arises. If you and the girls try your hand at Doing the Math and are able to convince others to join you, that's a big win for the girls and you, and for environmental justice. So get ready to start adding up some powerful numbers for justice.

WOMEN IN SPACE

On Oct. 25, 2007, some 200 miles above Earth, the Space Shuttle *Discovery* docked with the International Space Station, the hatches between the ships opened, and the two commanders followed standard NASA etiquette: They shook hands. But this handshake was one for the history books. The commanders of both missions were women: Pam Melroy and Peggy Whitson.

"It was no publicity stunt," says shuttle commander Melroy. Enough women had worked their way into leadership positions at NASA that a handshake like this was now possible.

Many more women work on the ground at NASA. Melroy recalls the women working on just one mission being called together for a photo. "Everyone was amazed and inspired when they realized the room was filled to nearly bursting!" she says.

> "The first woman to walk on Mars is in school today. Let's not let her down—let's help her get there."
>
> —Pam Melroy, commander, Space Shuttle *Discovery*

Ambassadors and the Great Outdoors

Justice is a big issue, but it's not the only focus of this journey. Be sure Ambassadors have opportunities to enjoy the wonders of the outdoors. As the Nature Break on page 7 of their book says:

> *At the heart of this journey is the belief that people everywhere should be able to enjoy the natural world and find health and strength in it. So take time to explore and enjoy the environment right outside your door, your school, your neighborhood, and your town. The journey's Nature Breaks give you new ways to strengthen your connection to the environment—and to have fun with your friends.*

By definition, Ambassadors are trailblazers, so when they venture outdoors, encourage them to travel far and wide. Any time spent in nature is bound to deepen their connections with the environment in a way that encourages lifelong stewardship of the planet.

Soar with the Birds

Justice invites lofty ideals and also offers some interesting inspirations from birds. The Ambassadors might like to go birding—and, in the process, visit someplace they've never been before.

Most regions have sanctuaries, refuges, and other special places to observe birds, so there's bound to be a place within reach where girls would enjoy exploring birds in their natural habitat. Check in with local bird clubs and birding enthusiasts. You might even find a few people willing to come along on the excursion.

Be sure the girls take note of all the interesting bird facts and bird behaviors mentioned throughout their book, too. While out birding, encourage them to consider all that birds and Ambassadors have in common!

Cover Art as Inspiration

If the girls want to put a creative spin on their outdoor adventures, perhaps they would enjoy making some photographs, watercolors, or other artistic creations while out and about.

Encourage the girls to take a close look at the cover and first page of their book, where they'll see how the cutout letters that form the word *JUSTICE* give way to images of injustice. Could they create the same see-through effect with images from their corner of the world? (See Session 5, page 85, for more ideas on how this cover art might inspire the Ambassadors.)

Or maybe they can find some local land decisions being made right now and get out to visit the sites. Is there land they might work to protect? Are there any NIMBYs or LULUs going on that they can explore (see page 29 in the girls' book)?

Camp Out

Nothing sets the mood for idealism like unplugging and enjoying the sights, sounds, and smells of the outdoors. Tastes count, too—the Ambassadors will enjoy planning meals cooked by a campfire (or solar cooker) that do justice to their thoughts! So check with your Girl Scout council for information about camping and camp facilities in your area, and then head out for some weekend retreats. Or explore state and national parks in your region. You might even go on a hike, during which the girls can share and debate solutions for environmental injustices.

Ceremonies and Traditions

Even the briefest of ceremonies can take girls away from the everyday to think about hopes, intentions, commitments, and feelings. A ceremony marks a separation from whatever girls have just come from (school, work, dance class, math club) and creates the sense that what happens to them—together, as Girl Scout Ambassadors—is special and important. So, find out how and when girls want ceremonies.

Girl Scout ceremonies can be as simple as gathering in a circle, lighting a candle, and sharing one hope—or reflecting together on one line of the Girl Scout Law. Or girls might read poems, play music, or sing songs. Invite them to create their own ways to mark their time together as special.

SING SOME SONGS!

Whether around a fire or just spontaneously in any location, singing is a great Girl Scout tradition. And so many songs speak of justice.

The girls might link up with other Ambassadors journeying to *JUSTICE* and have a sing-along that lifts up some hope. That's what this journey is all about!

World Thinking Day

The Ambassadors might devote this special day in Girl Scouting (February 22) to thinking about injustices around world—and how Girl Scouts and Girl Guides are making a difference.

Girl Scout Gold Award

Earning the Girl Scout Gold Award is an important tradition in Girl Scouting—and a great way to demonstrate leadership. Encourage girls to read about the award and girls who have earned it at girlscouts.org. They might ask their council to put them in touch with some of the young women who have earned it before them, so they can receive advice firsthand.

Ambassadors may also enjoy opportunities to educate and inspire younger girls. They might go birding together or simply share their favorite line from the Girl Scout Law. Whatever they do, encourage them to follow the Girl Scout motto: Be Prepared!

Connecting with Family, Friends, and an Ever-Growing Circle

Girl Scout Ambassadors will likely want to take trips and stay up late on retreats, and they may have a slew of fun ideas for the journey that they might like assistance with. Just remember, you don't have to be their only partner. Invite the girls' families and friends to get involved. Most important, encourage the girls themselves to think about who they can tap into. Mobilizing others, after all, is important when striving for justice!

The girls might also expand their network by reaching across the region to other Girl Scout Ambassadors taking this *JUSTICE* journey. For example, girls from distinct areas—rural, suburban, and urban—might come together to share their equations for justice. They'll see how issues of justice overlap or vary from one setting to another. And when teams of girls from various racial, ethnic, and socioeconomic groups can share ideas, whether online or in life, they all stand to benefit. The Ambassadors will see how to think bigger about the collective power of their efforts, even when Doing the Math.

PLAN AHEAD

Thinking ahead to the journey's final session, check in early with the girls to see if they'd like to plan a celebratory event that lets their families and friends share their accomplishments on this journey to justice.

Expert Voices

Also think ahead with the girls about experts in the community who might add value to the journey, and plan ahead for visits with them. For example, environmental experts and journalists can help with looking at issues from various perspectives, and other experts in the community could offer the girls perspectives on a range of careers, as suggested in Sessions 4 and 7.

Travel

Travel is a big part of Girl Scouting. Encourage the girls to check out the *destinations* program of travel opportunities at girlscouts.org. For international travel, the World Association of Girl Guides and Girl Scouts (WAGGGS) offers a wealth of opportunities. This umbrella organization for our worldwide sisterhood, founded in 1928, advocates globally on issues of importance to girls and young women.

What + How: Creating a Quality Experience

It's not just what girls do, but how you engage them that creates a high-quality experience. All Girl Scout activities are built on three processes that make Girl Scouting unique from school and other extracurricular activities. When used together, these processes—Girl Led, Cooperative Learning, and Learning by Doing (also known as Experiential Learning)—ensure the quality and promote the fun and friendship so integral to Girl Scouting. Take some time to understand these processes and how to use them with Girl Scout Ambassadors.

KEEP IT GIRL LED

Remember: You want the girls to take a major role in planning and executing this leadership experience. They may first want you to come up with the ideas and plans. But hold your ground! This is the girls' experience, and they're up to the challenge.

From beginning to end, keep your eye on what the girls want to do and the direction they seem to be taking. It's the approach begun by Juliette Gordon Low: When she and her associates couldn't decide on a new direction, she often said, "Let's ask the girls!" At each session, ask the girls for any last thoughts on what they've done or discussed!

Girl Led

"Girl led" is just what it sounds like—girls play an active part in figuring out the what, where, when, how, and why of their activities. So encourage them to lead the planning, decision-making, learning, and fun as much as possible, especially at this highest level of Girl Scouting. This ensures that girls are engaged in their learning and experience leadership opportunities as they prepare to become active participants in their local and global communities. With Ambassadors, you could:

- encourage girls to ask questions and independently identify challenges in neighborhoods, communities, and the world
- assist girls in developing connections with other girls, adults, and organizations on national and international levels
- assist girls in finding the resources they need to plan for their future careers

Learning by Doing

Learning by Doing is a hands-on learning process that engages girls in continuous cycles of action and reflection that result in deeper understanding of concepts and mastery of practical skills. As they participate in meaningful activities and then reflect on them, girls get to explore their own questions, discover answers, gain new skills, and share ideas and observations with others. Throughout the process, it's important for girls to be able to connect their experiences to their lives and apply what they have learned to their future experiences both within and outside of Girl Scouting. With Ambassadors, you could:

- support girls' learning by encouraging their participation in and leadership of challenging local or global community projects
- expose girls to a variety of people and experiences within and outside of Girl Scouting to use as resources for learning opportunities on local and global levels
- encourage girls to spend time talking about what they have learned from their experiences and to apply their insights to new opportunities

LEARNING BY DOING

It's not all "doing." Girls need time to talk between the action, so they can really capture what their experiences have taught them and keep on growing!

That's why you'll see discussion starters and suggested questions you can use with the girls in every sample session along the journey.

Cooperative Learning

Through cooperative learning, girls work together toward shared goals in an atmosphere of respect and collaboration that encourages the sharing of skills, knowledge, and learning. Moreover, given that many girls desire to connect with others, cooperative learning may be a particularly meaningful and enjoyable way to engage girls in learning. Working together in all-girl environments also encourages girls to feel powerful and emotionally and physically safe, and it allows them to experience a sense of belonging even in the most diverse groups. With Ambassadors, you could:

- engage girls in in-depth discussions about how cooperative learning is important, especially for girls and women
- expose girls to possible opportunities to teach or guide others in learning in cooperative ways
- encourage girls' to think and talk about their teamwork—and how they can use their teamwork skills in other settings

Seeing Girl Scout Processes Play Out in *JUSTICE*

Girl Scout processes play out in a variety of ways during team gatherings, but often they are so seamless you might not notice them. For example, in Session 2, the Ambassadors map out a local environmental justice issue by taking a birds-eye view. The call-outs below show how the Girl Scout processes make this a learning and growing experience for girls—and up the fun, too! Throughout *JUSTICE*, you'll see processes and outcomes play out again and again. Before you know it, you'll be using these valuable aspects of Girl Scouting in whatever Ambassadors do—from going for the Girl Scout Gold Award to traveling abroad to Girl Scout Cookie Activities!

FROM SAMPLE SESSION 2

Option: Map Out a Local Issue

The Ambassadors might want to dive in deeper to investigate a place or an emerging local issue, such as a landfill, factory, or power plant in their own region—by scoping out a birds-eye view.

The local news is a good place to start. Where is land being cleared to build something new? Who decided? Perhaps there are decisions pending that influence park lands or waste management. Girls can research the location of the problem and then map it in order to see where it is located with respect to residential and business neighborhoods. Who is being impacted? Who has not been involved in the decision? What LULUs and NIMBYs are in motion?

This is an excellent example of girls focused on a **Take Action** outcome within the **Girl Led** process. Here, girls are determining which issue in their community is in need of attention. This is in line with the **Take Action outcome, Girls identify community needs.** Once they have determined the need, they engage in the **Girl Led** process to research the issue to get a better understanding of the underlying or "root cause" of the problem.

Here, through their research, girls are also starting to ask questions that challenge and expand their thinking prior to their investigation. This broad critical thinking is the focus of the **Discover outcome, Girls develop critical thinking skills**, and is at the heart of the "bird's-eye view" approach to issues!

Encourage the Ambassadors to check out the Web site Scorecard.org, where they can type in their ZIP code and see how their county stacks up in terms of polluters, chemicals released, and industrial facilities. Is lead poisoning common in their community? Are there Superfund sites nearby? Scorecard allows the public to find out how much air pollution is released in their community, how clean the water is in nearby rivers and lakes. It also provides environmental justice reports for the community.

Here are some other ways to coach the girls along on their effort to get a bird's-eye view of a local issue:

- The Ambassadors will need to determine what resources they can use to assemble their map. Encourage them to discuss where they might find information about the location of landfills, industrial facilities, and water treatment plants. Libraries and municipal planning departments are usually the best places to start.
- Suggest that the girls include in their maps information about how these sites are connected to the rest of the city by roads, highways, waterways, and neighborhoods.
- The girls will find more information about zoning and controversies over LULUs (see page 29 in the girls' book), as well as the challenge of determining environmental risk, in the "Take the Scientific View" section of their book, beginning on page 72.

Suggest that once girls have explored their environmental issue in a local library, they might also find it helpful and interesting to contact sources in city government. Government bureaucracies can be hard to penetrate and girls may not find exactly what they are looking for right away. So here are some tips to offer:

- Local telephone directories will list city, county, state, and U.S. government offices.
- Most municipal governments have an environmental affairs information office that will be a good place to begin. But perhaps an even more effective approach would be to contact a representative from a local, regional, or state environmental group. Lois Gibbs, whose involvement in the Love Canal issue is described in page 19 of the girls' book, is head of the Center for Health, Environment and Justice, an organization she founded in 1981 that has provided resources, assistance, and training to more than 8,000 community groups. Similar organizations exist across the country, and girls can find their names and contact information online.

This suggestion recognizes two outcomes simultaneously. The girls' investigations have led to such an interest in their local communities that they feel compelled to act. This is an indicator that they are moving toward the **Connect outcome, Girls feel connected to their communities, locally and globally.** That girls are also reaching out to local government to learn more in order to address the problems means that they are actively seeking partnerships with community members to achieve greater participation and impact on their projects. This is central to the Ambassador-level **Take Action outcome, Girls are resourceful problem solvers.**

Understanding the Journey's Leadership Benefits

Filled with fun and friendship, *JUSTICE* is designed to develop the skills and values girls need to be leaders now and as they grow. The journey's activities are designed to enable Ambassadors to strive toward achieving 11 of 15 national outcomes, or benefits, of the Girl Scout Leadership Experience, as summarized on the next page. Each girl is different, so don't expect them all to exhibit the same signs to indicate what they are learning along the journey. What matters is that you are guiding them toward leadership skills and qualities they can use right now—and all their lives.

For full definitions of the outcomes and the signs that Girl Scout Ambassadors are achieving them, see *Transforming Leadership: Focusing on Outcomes of the New Girl Scout Leadership Experience* (GSUSA, 2008). Keep in mind that the intended benefits to girls are the cumulative result of traveling through an entire journey—and everything else girls experience in Girl Scouting.

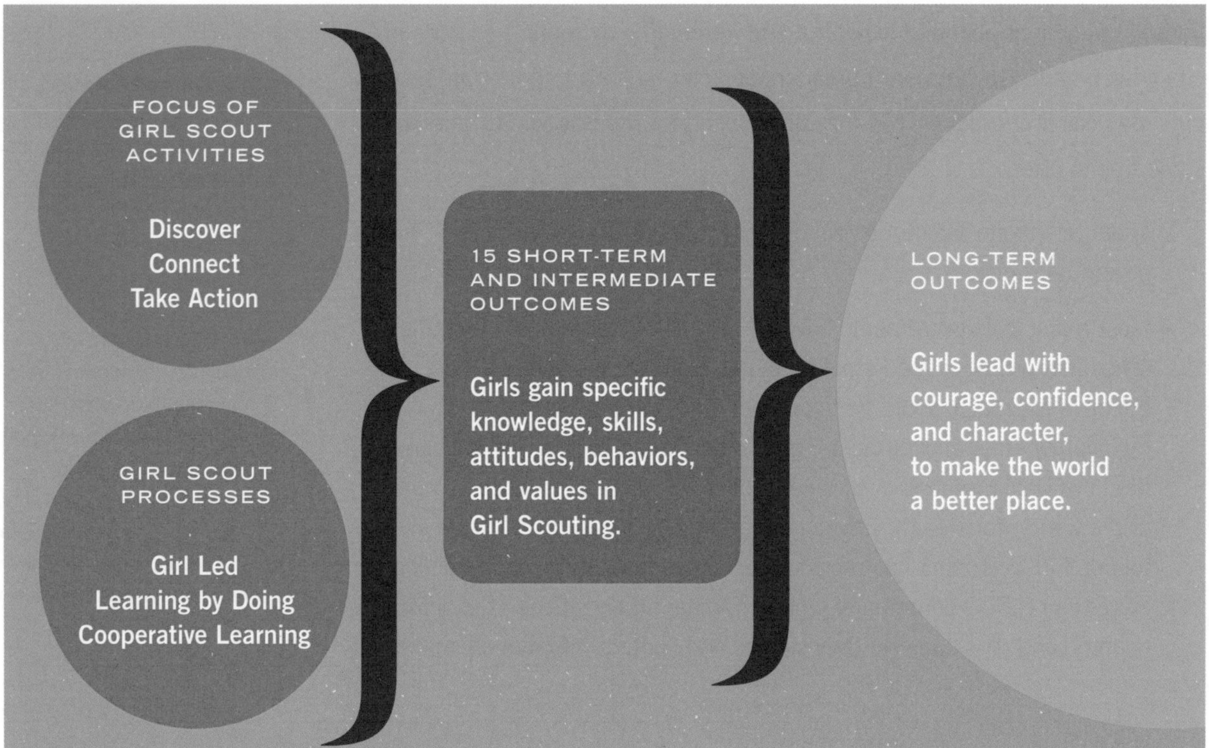

NATIONAL LEADERSHIP OUTCOMES

		AT THE AMBASSADOR LEVEL, girls...	RELATED ACTIVITIES (by Session number or girls' book page)	SAMPLE INDICATORS/SIGNS (when the outcome is achieved, girls might . . .
DISCOVER	Girls develop a strong sense of self.	feel they are better equipped to pursue future/life goals.	S4, S7, S9	report that they have options and possibilities for life/career goals.
	Girls develop positive values.	act consistently with a considered and self-determined set of values.	S3: Guilty Habits, Math; S4: Math; S6: I Changed My Mind, Check the Math; S8: Check the Math; GB: Hot on Campus, pp. 90–91	choose educational and career goals in line with the values they consider important.
		demonstrate commitment to promoting sustainable solutions to problems.	S1: Opening, Simple List; S2: Start Your E; S4, S5, S6: Add It In; S8: Opening; GB: Hearts & Minds; and pp. 9, 15–16, 22–23, 46; 47–49, 69, 101	report increased interest in making a sustainable impact beyond their local communities.
	Girls seek challenges in the world.	increasingly set challenging goals for the future.	S5: Opening Ceremony	see themselves in roles previously considered unattainable.
		have increased confidence to discuss and address challenging issues and contradictions in their lives and in their communities.	S1: Ranking; S2: Bird's-Eye; S3: Math; S4: Beyond the Hype; Get Dramatic; S5: Interviews; Whose Opinion; S6: Interview a DM; GB: pp. 38–41, 45–65	look for ways personal habits conflict with achieving goals.
			GB: pp. 17–19, 32–33, 34–35, 36–37	learn more about an issue from someone who has experienced injustice.
CONNECT	Girls promote cooperation and team building.	recognize the value of cooperation and team building for leadership and careers.	S1: Team Plans and Goals; S2: Casing It Out, Making Choices; S3: Opening, Closing; S8 Presentation Prep; GB: pp. 26, 55, 88, 99, 96	report that cooperation and team building skills helped them in other spheres of their lives.
	Girls feel connected to their communities.	have extensive feelings of connection with their local and global communities.	S3: Surveying; S7, S8: Opening Ceremony; GB: Karen Panetta feature, p. 8; Look High, Look Wide, p. 25	report more positive attitudes toward different members of their communities.
	Girls can resolve conflicts.	are better able to develop their own approaches to conflict resolution	S4, S9	give examples of how they adapted conflict-resolution strategies to personal situations.
TAKE ACTION	Girls can identify community needs.	are more skilled in identifying issues that balance feasibility with long-term change.	S2: Map It Out; S3: Surveying; S4: Survey Says	identify community partners that can continue their project goals into the future.
		choose projects that aim to address deeper causes of issues in their communities.	S6: Tracking the Footprint of a Decision	interview staff and residents of a shelter to identify root cause of homelessness in the community.
	Girls are resourceful problem solvers.	are better able to independently plan, organize, and manage projects.	S5: Controversy Strikes; S6: Interview a Decision Maker; S7: The E; S8: Presentation Prep; GB: Toward the Sage, pp. 10–13; Start, Continue, and Add to Your E, pp. 43, 92, and 102	monitor their own progress and determine criteria for success.
	Girls advocate for themselves and others.	recognize they can take part in development of public policy.	S5: Whose Opinion Really Counts?	report increased in projects that promote positive social changes.
		seek partnerships with groups that aid advocacy efforts.	S7: Who Cares?	report working with organizations that share their advocacy goals.
	Girls educate and inspire others to act.	are better able to evaluate the effectiveness of their efforts to educate diverse audiences.	S3: Math, Add to the E; S7: E, Who Cares? S8: Tips; S10: Reflection; GB: Nest, p. 70; Tips, pp. 106–108	implement innovative ways to access hard-to-reach audiences.
			S7: Reaching Out; GB: Do the Math, p. 45	work with other organizations to spread their messages effectively.
	Girls feel empowered to make a difference.	feel capable of bettering the functioning of communities.	GB: Where Will You Take Your E?, p. 109	create an action plan that could include more young people in setting town priorities.
		feel their projects and ideas are valued.	S9: Inspiring Justice; S10: Sage Award	give examples of positive reports about their Take Action Projects.

S=Session; GB=Girls' book; math=Do the Math; E=Equation; DM=Decision-Maker; ECs= Environmental Citizens

From *Your Voice, Your World* to *JUSTICE*

If the Ambassadors have already journeyed through *Your Voice, Your World*, they'll find lots of ways to use their insights here in the search for justice. Here are just a few ideas to make the links:

Networking: The girls may find themselves tapping their allies and VIP contacts again. They can ask those they met to assist them to expand their network further—to find scientists, decision makers, and media contacts they need to talk to on this journey to earn the Sage Award!

Big Issues: The Ambassadors may have uncovered an issue to advocate for that relates to *JUSTICE*. If so, they could keep going with that issue, putting it through the steps to an equation for justice!

Personal Values and the Law: And of course they'll continue to look at their values—and those of the Girl Scout Law—in their search for justice.

Plus, if they had some fun with the "Take 5" activities in *Your Voice, Your World,* or started a ceremony or other traditions, by all means keep them going! How about a "J is for Justice" team poem along the lines of "A is for Ambassador"?

JUSTICE FIRST?

If the Ambassadors are doing this *JUSTICE* journey first, ahead of *Your Voice, Your World,* encourage them to keep track of issues they uncover that they would like to advocate for in order to influence change!

Then, when they start *Your Voice, Your World*, they'll have a great jumping-off point! Who knows, issues they explore may even point them to a Girl Scout Gold Award project!

Your Perspective on Leadership

The Girl Scout Leadership philosophy—Discover + Connect + Take Action—implies that leadership happens from the inside out. Your thoughts, enthusiasm, and approach will influence the Ambassadors, so take some time to reflect on your own perspective on leadership. Take a few minutes now—and throughout *Justice*—to apply the three "keys" of leadership to yourself.

Discover + Connect + Take Action = Leadership

DISCOVER **What values do you hold related to caring for the environment? Is it ever hard to act on them? Why? What does the Girl Scout Law line "use resources wisely" mean to you?**

____

____

____

CONNECT **Who would you like to add to your community network? Why do you think it's important for Ambassadors to connect with an expanding network of people?**

____

____

____

TAKE ACTION **How does your role as a volunteer with Girl Scout Ambassadors contribute to making the world—and specifically the environment—better?**

____

____

____

"I wanted to use the law to find solutions that took into account . . . many different perspectives . . . I try to sit at as many stones . . . as I can."

— Annie Petsonk, international counsel, Environmental Defense Fund

The Journey's 10 Sample Sessions

Embarking on this journey to *JUSTICE* is big! But these sample session plans, along with the girls' book, will guide you every step of the way. Keep in mind that sample is truly the key word here. You and the Ambassadors can tailor and tweak your gatherings as you like.

Begin by reading through the girls' book just to become familiar with all it holds. Its combination of inspirations and information will engage the girls (and you) in the many subthemes of this journey.

Keep in mind: There's no need to memorize anything. The session plans are set up to step the girls right through all the requirements to earning the prestigious Sage Award. They'll tell you what parts of the girls' book you might want to reference and they'll offer fun little extras and options—for food, art, and friendship—all along the way. There's plenty to get your imagination—and the imaginations of all the Ambassadors—soaring!

Just remember: There's no one route to justice. And being on a Girl Scout leadership journey is bigger and more important than any one activity on its own.

What You'll Find in Each Session

SUGGESTIONS, NOT MUST-DO'S

If you're wondering whether you "must" do each activity or ceremony, you can usually presume the answer is no! This guide is full of suggestions for ways to give girls the Girl Scout experience of leadership. Do what's best for the girls on your Ambassador team.

BE GREEN, KEEP MATERIALS HANDY

A box or bag with markers, pens, and scrap paper will prove handy to bring to the sessions. Perhaps girls and their families can help round up these basic supplies—leftovers will certainly do. If your meeting space has a chalkboard or newsprint and easel, that's great. Otherwise, have a few poster boards or sheets of newsprint handy. Or recycle file folders, use the backs of posters, and so on.

Several sessions suggest making photocopies of pages in this guide for the girls. But feel free to go green and cut back on paper use any way you can!

AT A GLANCE: The session's goal, activities, and a list of simple materials you'll need.

What to Say: Examples of what to say and ask the Ambassadors along *Justice* as you link activities, reflections, and learning experiences. Must you read from the "script"? Absolutely not! The girls (and you) will have far more fun if you take the main ideas from the examples provided and then just be yourself.

Activity Instructions: Tips for guiding the girls through activities and experiences along *Justice* and plenty of "tools" (lists, charts, suggestions for reflections, etc.) to correspond to the experiences on the journey.

Coaching to Create a Quality Experience: The quality of the Girl Scout Leadership Experience depends greatly on three processes—Girl Led, Learning by Doing, and Cooperative Learning. By following the prompts in this guide for activities, reflections, girl choice-making, and discussions, you'll be using the processes—with ease.

Tying Activities to Impact: This guide notes the purpose of the journey's activities and discussions, so you'll always understand the intended benefit to girls. You'll even be able to see the benefits—by observing the "signs" that the girls are achieving the national Girl Scout Leadership Outcomes.

Customizing the Journey

Keep in mind that this is a journey packed with activities, information, and enriching experiences. As you create a schedule with your group of Ambassadors, you and the girls may want to stretch out the journey over a longer period of time than the sample sessions in this guide suggest. You may find you need more sessions, or shorter sessions or fewer sessions—that's for you and the girls to decide!

Just encourage the girls to be creative about scheduling the journey. Time is set aside in Session 1 for just this purpose, and the *JUSTICE*: Make It Your Own pages (36–37 in this guide) will assist the girls in their planning.

Roadside Attractions

As time allows, encourage the girls to "get off the highway" whenever possible to enjoy their own "roadside attractions." Stops can be "business" or "pleasure." Here are a few ideas (the session plans, the girls' book, and the Ambassadors themselves will have even more):

- Find out what local environmental organizations are doing. Your Girl Scout council may also have ideas to offer.
- Discuss the pros and cons of a recent policy decision made at the local, state, or federal level. Maybe even conduct a debate. Why do the girls think the officials in charge decided as they did? What would the girls have done? Why? Maybe other Ambassadors in the region would like to join in!
- Visit places (such as a childhood home, nature preserves, or parks) that honor those who worked for environmental justice.

MAKE SOME STUFF

Girls who like to make things (crafts, recipes, do-it-yourself projects, inventions, crazy videos) will enjoy sharing their talents with the team. Encourage the girls to have fun as they share their favorite creative efforts. They can even exchange what they've made with each other. (Gifting ceremony, anyone?)

JUST HANGING OUT

There are no hard-and-fast rules about how much time Girl Scout Ambassadors spend exploring the topic of justice. Still, it's important to reserve some time for just hanging out. Emotional connections with other girls and a safe space to enjoy them are a key part of what makes Girl Scouting unique.

SAMPLE SESSION 1
Toward Justice

AT A GLANCE

Goal: Girls begin to think about what justice asks of each of us as individuals. They examine the ways in which environmental concerns can be ranked based on various needs and perspectives. They go on to explore how their desires for environmental justice compete with self-interests.

- **Opening Ceremony: Toward Justice**
- **A Simple List: What Really Matters?**
- **Team Plans and Goals**
- **Closing Ceremony: Vision**
- **Looking Ahead to Session 2**

MATERIALS

- A pad of newsprint, or a blackboard or whiteboard, and colored markers
- paper and pens or a computer

PREPARE AHEAD: CRAFT OPTION

Throughout the journey, the Ambassadors will capture ideas and insights that will aid them in developing their equation for justice. Depending on their interests, and time available, the girls might enjoy creating a journal, team mural, keepsake box, or other item to hold their ideas. This "Add-It-In Kit" can serve as a springboard to creating and presenting their equations as the journey nears its conclusion. If "getting crafty" appeals to the girls, plan time at an early gathering to make or decorate the chosen item. Encourage the girls to use recycled materials and to pool their supplies and creativity!

Opening Ceremony: Toward Justice

Write the last line of the Pledge of Allegiance on a large piece of paper or cardboard: "With liberty and justice for all." As girls arrive, gather the team in a circle around it.

Ask girls to think about a question that comes to mind when they consider this phrase. A few examples might include: What does justice ask of us? Who needs justice most? What would justice mean for Earth? Is it possible?

Encourage each girl to add her question to the paper. Add your own question, too. If this is a first-time gathering for the team, you might each introduce yourselves as you add your questions.

Next, ask the girls to read the opening line of their *JUSTICE* book:

> *"Through the ages and across the world, people have always yearned for justice. And yet justice—for Earth and all its inhabitants—continues to elude us."*

Ask girls what this line means to them. On the back of the page where the girls have written their questions about justice, encourage them to write a word or phrase that symbolizes what justice on Earth could look like. If girls have particular injustices in mind, ask them to express what the opposite of that injustice would look like.

LOOKING AHEAD, LOOKING BACK

Let the team know that toward the end of the journey, they'll revisit this two-sided "Toward Justice" sheet to see what new ideas and questions they've developed along the way.

Once each girl has written something, invite the Ambassador team to consider this question: *How does environmental justice go hand in hand with justice for people? What related examples can you think of?*

Then summarize the journey the girls are about to begin. You could include the following points, or whatever strikes you or the girls as important from the opening pages of their book:

- *A journey has a beginning and an end point. It is by crossing the distance between the two that we become a little wiser.*

LOST AND FOUND

Lots of artists today make incredible works of art from found objects (that means trash!) that they use in new ways.

Round up the Ambassadors and spend some time at a museum of art and design or folk art, or visit a craft show or craft exhibit, or a sculpture garden or other art space in your area and see how everything from bottle caps to cans to scrap metal can be re-purposed—with imagination.

Get the girls starting a team "treasure box" to collect whatever strikes their fancy—bottle caps, scrap paper, wrapping paper, bows, boxes, string.

Then make a date to get the girls' imaginations going! A checker game from cardboard, bottle tops, and fabric or paper scraps? Some little kid might love that! What else? An earring tree fashioned by punching holes in a can? An artifact that helps you present your equation for justice?

- *Along this journey, you will be creating your own unique definition and equation for justice: What does it mean for Earth and all of us, and how do we go about achieving it?*
- *Ultimately, you'll have a chance to share your vision for justice with whoever you think needs to hear it because once you can define justice, you can strive for it—and inspire others to do so, too.*
- *We can't create justice until we imagine it.*
- *Each of has a role and a stake in creating justice.*

Then wrap up the opening of the journey with some inspiration lines. Consider these lines (from a Latin American prayer) or something you and the girls like:

> *To those who have hunger, give bread;*
> *To those who have bread, give the hunger for justice.*

Ask the girls: *Do these words inspire you in any specific way as you begin this journey? How do they help frame your vision of justice?*

A Simple List: What Really Matters?

Is there any such thing as a "simple list" of environmental justice issues? That's the question at the heart of this exercise. As the girls explore issues from many perspectives, they deepen their understanding of the diversity of environmental concerns and self-interests that often hinder people's ability to act on them.

Creating a list is a great starting point for an exploration of how various concerns and self-interests may contribute to possible definitions of justice—and steps toward achieving justice.

Start by asking an Ambassador to write one thing she cares about in the environment on the board or a paper, or whatever your group has chosen to write its list on. Then invite each girl to add one thing until all the girls have had a chance to contribute to the list.

Girls may list general environmental themes, such as clean water, health, or biodiversity, or geographic categories like rain forests or coral reefs, or endangered animals like polar bears. They may also offer specific things they worry about, such as oil spills, melting glaciers, mountains of garbage, or air pollution. There's no need to stick to only broad or only specific concerns.

If the group is small or the Ambassadors have more ideas to share, invite them to continue adding to the list for another round. Continue until the girls have listed a dozen to two dozen issues.

Ranking the Cares and Concerns

Now ask the girls to get into teams of two or three girls to rank the list by priority. First, they'll have to come up with a system for ranking. Encourage them to discuss what considerations they should use to rank their priorities. You might offer these examples:

- *The most pressing or precious issue*
- *The deadliest threat*
- *Issues that affect the most people*
- *Concerns that affect particular groups, such as children, most severely*
- *Problems that could be most effectively reduced or eliminated*

The girls' thoughts may differ, so emphasize that there are no right answers. Encourage a good discussion about the girls' reasons for their ranking criteria before they actually rank the concerns. Then bring the mini-teams back together and have each team report on what it ranked as the top concerns and the criteria it used to come up with them. Guide a group discussion around the following questions:

- *How do your personal values influence what you prioritize?*
- *Is there "one right list"?*
- *When priorities compete, what wins out?*
- *Where do self-interests come into play?*

As the discussion wraps up, let the girls know that exploring which environmental justice issues really matter to whom is a theme they will investigate throughout this journey. Nearly everyone will say that the environment matters to them, but the specifics of what matters to each person tend to differ in dramatic ways. Wanting clean beaches, more parks, and better air quality are all environmental concerns, but so, too, are desires to end global warming and protect orangutans. You might close out by saying:

How do you know what's right? That's what our search for an equation for justice is all about!

THROUGH ANOTHER LENS

Time permitting, the girls could look at their list of concerns again, taking turns imagining themselves as various "officials." One girl might be the head of a major environmental group, the next could be the CEO of a large paper manufacturer, the third could be the U.S. president. Invite the girls to name their own official post. As this official, what are their top three priorities on the list and why?

Team Plans and Goals

Engage the girls in a team discussion about tailoring their *JUSTICE* experience to meet their needs, interests, and the time they have available. They can use copies of the planning sheets on the following pages to guide them as they think about how to customize their journey.

JUSTICE: Make It Your Own

THINK ABOUT . . .	WHAT WE'LL DO
THE SAGE AWARD: Are you interested in earning the award? What do you hope to learn and explore by doing so? Do you want to complete the award steps as individuals and discuss and share insights with the team? Or progress through the steps as a team? Use your gatherings primarily to work on the award, or mix in other opportunities along the way?	
FREESTYLING: You might opt to "mix and match" ideas from *JUSTICE* to create your own journey, and not focus on earning the Sage Award. What ideas from the Nest, Soar, and Puzzler sections of your book spark your interest? Perhaps you want to focus on exploring career ideas or use your energy on a particular topic covered in *JUSTICE*? There is no right or wrong way for your Ambassador team to journey through *JUSTICE*!	
CEREMONIES: What (if anything) would you like to do to mark your time together as special and apart from all the busyness of life? Would you enjoy a chance to tell one another a good thing and a challenge you have experienced in life between Ambassador gatherings? Would you like to practice a few minutes of quiet together, aided by a candle, music, or a beautiful photo from nature? Take turns sharing poems and quotes? A blend of these? None of these? Note that the sample sessions in your adult volunteer's guide offer ceremony ideas, too. Again, the best solution is the one you and your sister Ambassadors create for yourselves—and this might even include "winging it" from session to session!	
CAREER EQUATIONS: During your search for an equation for justice, you can add in time to build an equation, or two or 10, about your future. You and your teammates might visit a university to interview some "science-y" people (a step to the Sage). You can also stop at the financial-aid office, take a tour, and check out the dorms! Multitask your way through every step to the Sage—something for "justice," something for you! Think about how the two come together. Now that's being sage!	

JUSTICE: Make It Your Own

THINK ABOUT . . .	WHAT WE'LL DO
CONFLICT SOLUTIONS: As you build your equation for justice, you'll see that some of the issues you explore might be useful in resolving conflicts in your personal life, too! You'll hear more about this in your team gatherings, but you may have your own ideas about this, too. If you are especially interested in getting better at solving the kinds of daily conflicts that come up between friends, at school, or at home, think about taking some time to dig deeper. You might seek out tips from a mediator, counselor, lawyer, or judge.	
ADDITIONAL LEADERSHIP OPPORTUNITIES: Perhaps you and other Ambassadors (or each in turn!) would like to take charge of guiding the exploration and discussion ideas provided in your adult volunteer's guide (tailoring and tweaking and making them your own as you go). Choose a session and "sign on" to lead. When your session is coming up, chat with your adult volunteer to get assistance in thinking the gathering through and adding your own creative touches.	
ENJOYING THE GREAT OUTDOORS: How would you like to spend some time in nature? Day hikes? A weekend camping retreat? Maybe your team can even link up with other Ambassador groups exploring *JUSTICE* and make it a mega-campout with time to share ideas and networks. Check out inspirational tidbits about birds throughout your book. How about visiting a bird sanctuary or a wildlife refuge?	
NETWORKING: Who would you like to talk to as you journey? Members of a local zoning and planning board? The person developing an environmental impact statement for a local building project? Epidemiologists? Volunteers at a nature preserve or environmental action organization? Building a network of people will enrich your journey—and give you ideas and resources for college and career planning! Start early by pooling the team's ideas and connections!	

Closing Ceremony: Vision

Share this information with the girls: *Arctic terns and sooty shearwaters fly between 25,000 miles and 40,000 miles each in their migration back and forth between their Arctic breeding grounds and the Antarctic. In the birds' lifetimes, that's the equivalent of flying to the Moon and back!*

While the shearwaters' main flyway traces a huge figure eight over the Pacific Ocean, most terns fly in an oval pattern over the Atlantic Ocean, but some fly down the Pacific coast as well. The birds time their migration so they spend summer in the northern polar region and then fly to the southern polar region to enjoy summer there, too.

This means that not only do the birds cover the planet top to bottom in their migration, but they also see more daylight than any creature in the world. Talk about the perfect bird's-eye view of the planet!

Ask the Ambassador team to reflect on the importance of vision, using questions like these:

- *If you could see as much of the Earth in daylight as the shearwaters and terns, what would you want to see? What would make you happy? What would make you sad?*
- *How can a sharp inner vision contribute to creating justice? What happens when we have no vision?*
- *What is possible when our inner visions, values, and goals are lined up in pursuit of justice?*

Looking Ahead to Session 2

If the team wants to try the Opening Ceremony suggested for the next session, invite the girls to bring in a photo, postcard, poster, or magazine illustration about nature or an actual object from nature—anything that shows something on Planet Earth they care about.

PERSONAL GOALS COUNT, TOO!

Keep an ear out for opportunities to encourage girls to identify and pursue personal goals. Possible discussion starters could include:

- *How do you know when your interests or plans or passions become a goal?*
- *Has a goal ever snuck up on you, and if it has, how did that happen?*
- *How do your personal values shape your goals, and does it work the other way around, too?*
- *Has a family member or friend ever suggested a goal to you, and have you ever done the same?*
- *How have your goals grown or shrunk or changed dramatically?*
- *And if you really want to stick with a commitment, what's the best goal glue you've found?*

Invite girls to consider how they might want to incorporate an ongoing discussion of personal goals into the journey.

SAMPLE SESSION 2

Look High, Look Wide

AT A GLANCE

Goal: Girls find ways to see the big picture of environmental justice issues. As they explore what it means to "sit at every stone" in search for justice, they also consider how a "high and wide" perspective can help them resolve conflicts in their own relationships.

- **Opening Ceremony: Nature We Care About**
- **Telling a Story from a Bird's-Eye View**
- **Casing It Out: Sit at Every Stone**
- **Option: Map Out a Local Issue**
- **Start Your Equation**
- **Closing Ceremony: Conflicts and You**
- **Looking Ahead to Session 3**

MATERIALS

- **Opening Ceremony:** images provided by the girls
- **Telling a Story:** Two dozen printed images from online photo sources or old magazines, glued or taped to large index cards or pieces of cardboard

PREPARE AHEAD

Seek out a pair of Ambassadors to organize the materials ahead of time for the "Telling a Story from a Bird's-Eye View" activity. They'll need to find two dozen photos that can be used to tell a variety of stories. That may sound a bit mysterious—and complicated—but here's how it works: The girls will use the photos like a deck of cards, arranging them in a sequence to tell a story.

Photos can be clipped from old magazines, or the girls can tap online sources and print photos from a specific historical period. Google Images, for example, now includes millions of photos from the LIFE archive that can be used for personal, non-commercial purposes. Pick a decade—the 1880s or the 1930s, perhaps—and then choose and print two dozen images that show interesting people, settings, and action. The girls might even find some photos already arranged in sequences. A home computer and printer, or one at the local library, will produce quality images on ordinary printer paper. The girls can tape or glue the images to index cards or pieces of lightweight cardboard and then number the photos on the back, from 1 to 24.

Opening Ceremony: Nature We Care About

Ask the girls to gather around with the items they brought in that are about or from nature. Each girl can briefly describe her item and why she chose it. With any luck, it will be a diverse collection!

Ask the girls to consider all of the places represented by their photos and objects. Explain that a key challenge in building an equation for justice is always looking for the big picture—the larger context in which environmental injustices develop. But it is often difficult to get above it all in order to achieve that much-needed bird's-eye view.

Telling a Story from a Bird's-Eye View

Have the girls divide into two teams. Give one team the two dozen story cards. Then give them 10 minutes to brainstorm together. Their goal is to choose 12 pictures and create a sequential story with them. The girls will dream up their story and order the photos in sequence, but not show the other team (the numbers on the back of the photo cards will help them remember the order).

The first team will then give the photos to the second team, along with two hints: the first and last photos of their story. The second team now has 10 minutes to try to lay out the first team's story.

When they're done, ask the girls questions like:

- *Did you expect the two story versions to match up better or worse than they did?*
- *How many stories could be told with the same dozen photos?*
- *What makes it hard to predict the other team's story?*
- *What sort of stories would you expect from younger girls or older women using the same 12 photos?*

HOW'S YOUR NEST?

Ask the girls to think about the place they call home. What do they have—possessions, habits, or routines—that makes life more convenient? A TV in every room? Ditto for computers or music-playing devices? Habits like buying clothes they wear only once or twice? Or the newest cell phone, even though the old one was just fine? Do they ask for a ride when they could walk or bike?

Get the Ambassadors thinking about the conveniences they would you give up if they knew it could ultimately contribute to solving an injustice somewhere on Earth. Ask:

How hard is it to give something up? Try it! While you're at it, ponder this: What are people willing to give up, in a big way, to save Earth and all her inhabitants? What stops people from pitching in?

Instead of buying new clothes, how about "shopping your own closet" and making cool new outfits from old stuff, or raiding your mom's jewelry box and borrowing a broach or clunky bracelet to jazz up an outfit?

- *What stories would you expect from boys or men, girls from Africa or Asia, or individuals from very poor or very wealthy communities?*

Transition the team into a broader discussion about how easy it is to forget that we each see the world from a unique perspective—our own! You might say: *Even when we agree on the basics of something simple, like a school trip, we will likely emphasize different things and have a different interpretation of people, places, and events. That's human nature!*

Wrap up by inviting the team to consider some of these questions:

- *Why is it so important to try to see situations from as many perspectives as possible?*
- *How do we piece together stories when we don't have all the information?*
- *How does taking a bird's-eye view of an environmental problem expand your view of injustice?*
- *How could seeing various sides of a story help resolve the injustice or avoid a future injustice?*

Casing It Out: Sit at Every Stone

Ask the team to check out the profile of Annie Petsonk, international counsel for the Environmental Defense Fund, on page 27 of their book.

Then ask: *How would the principle of "sitting at every stone" contribute to more justice in the world?*

Now ask the team to check out the section "A Movement Emerges," beginning on page 15 of their book. Then start a discussion based on these questions: *Who was not involved in the decision-making? Who forgot to "sit at every stone?" What was the result? Who was most affected?*

The Ambassadors can continue their exploration of "sitting at every stone" by checking out the various "case studies" in their book, choosing those that most interest them. If the group is large, the girls might like to "divvy up" and analyze the cases in mini-teams and then report back to the full group.

As they analyze and discuss the cases, you might suggest that the girls consider the questions in "Start Your Equation," on page 42 of their book.

The girls may be ready to "check off" the "Look High, Look Wide" step toward the Sage Award after this gathering, or they might decide to research and discuss more cases.

Option: Map Out a Local Issue

The Ambassadors might want to dive in deeper to investigate a place or an emerging local issue, such as a landfill, factory, or power plant in their own region—by scoping out a birds-eye view.

The local news is a good place to start. Where is land being cleared to build something new? Who decided? Perhaps there are decisions pending that influence park lands or waste management. Girls can research the location of the problem and then map it in order to see where it is located with respect to residential and business neighborhoods. Who is being impacted? Who has not been involved in the decision? What LULUs and NIMBYs are in motion?

Encourage the Ambassadors to check out the Web site Scorecard.org, where they can type in their ZIP code and see how their county stacks up in terms of polluters, chemicals released, and industrial facilities. Is lead poisoning common in their community? Are there Superfund sites nearby? Scorecard allows the public to find out how much air pollution is released in their community, how clean the water is in nearby rivers and lakes. It also provides environmental justice reports for the community.

Here are some other ways to coach the girls along on their effort to get a bird's-eye view of a local issue:

- The Ambassadors will need to determine what resources they can use to assemble their map. Encourage them to discuss where they might find information about the location of landfills, industrial facilities, and water treatment plants. Libraries and municipal planning departments are usually the best places to start.
- Suggest that the girls include in their maps information about how these sites are connected to the rest of the city by roads, highways, waterways, and neighborhoods.
- The girls will find more information about zoning and controversies over LULUs (see page 29 in the girls' book), as well as the challenge of determining environmental risk, in the "Take the Scientific View" section of their book, beginning on page 72.

Placing an environmental issue in a larger context can help frame questions about the issue. Encourage girls to ask questions like these:

- *What does the map reveal about the factors that might have been considered in locating the landfills or other facilities?*
- *When was the decision to build the landfill (or factory or power plant) made, and which people were involved in the decision?*
- *Was there a vote by residents of the city?*
- *Did newspapers and local media cover the decision when it was made?*
- *Was there opposition to the decision?*

Suggest that once girls have explored their environmental issue in a local library, they might also find it helpful and interesting to contact sources in city government. Government bureaucracies can be hard to penetrate and girls may not find exactly what they are looking for right away. So here are some tips to offer:

- Local telephone directories will list city, county, state, and U.S. government offices.
- Most municipal governments have an environmental affairs office that will be a good place to begin. But perhaps an even more effective approach would be to contact a representative from a local, regional, or state environmental group. Lois Gibbs, whose involvement in the Love Canal issue is described on page 19 of the girls' book, is head of the Center for Health, Environment and Justice, an organization she founded in 1981 that has provided resources, assistance, and training to more than 8,000 community groups. Similar organizations exist across the country, and girls can find their names and contact information online.

If the girls become interested in an emerging local issue, they can focus on it to shape the rest of the steps toward the SAGE Award, and their culminating presentation. For example, they can examine the media coverage (or lack thereof) to achieve Step 3 (Be HAWK-EYED), drill down on a scientific aspect of the issue to reach Step 4 (Take the SCIENTIFIC View), and talk to decision-makers and those with influence to reach Step 5 (DECIPHER Decisions). They might complement the information they've found with time lines, graphics, video clips, or photographs that help tell their story.

Start Your Equation

When the girls are ready to start capturing their definition and equation for justice, begin with a quick overview of "Add It Up: Your Equation for Justice," beginning on page 11 of their book.

> **TIMING IS EVERYTHING**
>
> Your team might be ready to start their equations at this gathering. If not, do this overview at another time.

To get the group focused, write "Justice" on a large sheet of paper or a chalkboard. Then ask:

- *What are some parts of the equation, and the definition of justice, that are becoming clear to you?*

Encourage the girls to capture any phrases and ideas that are on their minds, individually and as a team. If the girls have created a "crafty way" to capture their ideas, now's the time to start using it. Otherwise, scratch paper is just fine!

If the group has a hard time getting started, you might offer these reminders about the ground the team has already covered:

- *How does a bird's-eye view help?*
- *What does it mean to sit at every stone?*
- *What happens when you skip a stone?*
- *What actions, decisions, habits, or assumptions caused some of the injustices we have analyzed?*
- *What steps could be in an equation to prevent them?*

Closing Ceremony: Conflicts and You

Encourage the Ambassadors to apply "Look High, Look Wide" to resolving conflicts in their own lives. Get started by asking: *What are examples of times when you have been stuck in a conflict with others? Think about a current conflict you need to resolve.*

Get the girls talking about how "sitting at every stone" can be a useful tool in conflict resolution. You might ask:

- *Have you ever experienced a conflict that moved to resolution because someone was able to shift her perspective?*
- *What happens if no one is able to shift?*
- *Why is it so hard to "give up your own perspective" to take on another one? What strategies can you think of to push yourself and others to consider various perspectives as a way to resolve conflicts constructively?*

Ask girls if they would like to try making a commitment to practicing "sitting at every stone" over the next several weeks when they find themselves in the midst of a conflict among family or friends.

Close with a short go-round, in which each girl fills in this line:

The practice of sitting at every stone would help me . . .

Looking Ahead to Session 3

At the next gathering, the Ambassadors will think about using math creatively, as they select and commit to a personal action that can have a positive impact on environmental justice. You might ask if anyone knows a fun math or science teacher who might like to join in.

Also encourage the girls to get their creative juices flowing on how they might ultimately capture and present their definition of justice and an equation for bringing it about. What talents and skills do they have (or want to develop)—photography, video, music, visual art, poetry, writing, or . . . ?

They don't have to decide right now, but they might want to start experimenting and begin bringing in supplies and possibilities to use at upcoming sessions. They might "get creative" a little bit at a time at each gathering, or choose to wait until they have finished their definition and equation (using words, pen and paper, etc.), and then devote a stretch of time to getting creative about presenting it.

SAMPLE SESSION 3
Do the Math

AT A GLANCE

Goal: Girls identify ways to lighten their step on the planet and make a commitment to follow through and record their results. They explore how "doing the math" can be an effective motivation and communication tool in the quest for environmental justice. They also create a simple survey to explore what other people believe about environmental issues, and what actions they are willing to take to contribute to change.

- **Opening Ceremony: Overcoming Resistance**
- **Guilty Habits**
- **Do the Math!**
- **Surveying for More Perspectives**
- **Add to the Equation!**
- **Closing Ceremony: Hope and Despair**
- **Looking Ahead to Session 4**

MATERIALS

- **Opening Ceremony:** A lightweight 6-foot (or longer) balsawood stick (available at craft supply stores), bamboo garden stake, or thin hollow plastic tube The lighter the better, as this is the "levitation stick"!
- **Do the Math:** Copies of examples, pages 52–53
- **Surveying for More Perspectives:** Copies of "Writing Surveys: Tips and Examples," page 56; "Simple List(s)" created during Session 1; paper and pens or markers; computer for writing survey (optional)

PREPARE AHEAD

A math or statistics teacher or expert would be a fun addition to this session, so if the girls recommended one at the end of the last session, make sure they've followed through on an invitation.

TIMING IS EVERYTHING

The Ambassadors are likely finding that resistance is a key factor when trying to change habits to bring about justice—especially when one is trying to get a group to move in the same direction at the same time.

This activity puts a fun spin on this challenge and gives the girls a chance to do some team building, too!

Opening Ceremony: Overcoming Resistance

Ask for one or two girls to volunteer as referees. Then divide the remaining Ambassadors into two groups and have them line up shoulder to shoulder in two rows, facing each other, three feet apart.

- Have them raise both arms, waist high, with their index (pointer) fingers extended toward, but a few inches to the left or right of, the index fingers of the girls facing them.
- Lay the lightweight "levitation stick" (see Materials, page 43) on top of all the extended fingers. Make sure the stick is in contact with all of the girls' index fingers. If there are a dozen girls, the stick will now be resting on 24 index fingers. It will look a bit like a caterpillar with girls attached!
- Then tell the girls that the goal of the group is to lower the levitation stick all the way to the ground while NEVER losing contact with any of the girls' index fingers. If any girl loses contact with the stick with her index finger, the group starts the challenge over at waist height.

The referee's job is to be vigilant about finger contact! Just one slip and the game is restarted.

It sounds easy. But what happens is that the harder the girls try to get the stick to the ground, the more the stick stubbornly keeps rising, in defiance of the group's goal. The girls may laugh, but the stick keeps levitating. How come?

VALUES VERSUS SELF-INTEREST

Many of us know that we should waste less paper, avoid plastic bags and bottles, and walk more and drive less. Yet we allow our busyness and our habits of convenience to excuse us from making even small changes that could add up to have an impact on Earth. What we value is in conflict with our self-interest!

Here's a chance for the Ambassadors to create a little more justice in the world, based on a commitment to "do the math," change a habit, and maybe even get some others to do the same.

The reason is that the upward pressure from all the index fingers desperately trying to maintain contact with the stick is greater than the downward pressure of the weight of the stick. The result is levitation against the will of the girls!

After several tries, ask the girls to consider their strategies. What approach might improve their progress? It takes concentration, communication, and teamwork to gently bring the stick to the ground.

If they succeed, invite them to explain what the key to their success was. If they don't manage to bring the stick all the way to the ground, ask them what they think would be required to do so. *Is it impossible? What would need to change? Can you see any parallels with anything else in your lives and on this journey that reminds you of the levitation stick?*

Guilty Habits

Ask the girls to consider the word "lifestyle." It can mean many different things to different people. But in the most fundamental sense, it is the sum total of our decisions.

Get the girls thinking by asking a few questions like these:

- *How do our actions, even what we eat and drink, support or conflict with our environmental values?*
- *How do our daily decisions, our lifestyle, relate to injustices? How many small decisions stacked up together create injustice?*
- *How do daily decisions intersect with, or conflict with, what we say we care about?*

Invite the girls to gather around. On a large piece of paper or cardboard each girl can write one "guilty habit" that goes against what she values and knows is good for the Earth. You might write one, too! If anyone is struggling, flip through the girls' book for ideas. (Bottled water anyone? Trash full of . . . ? What else?)

When everyone has had a chance to write a guilty habit, engage in a team discussion about why we hang on to habits that go against our concern of caring for Earth. A few questions for this conversation might include:

- *When convenience or self-interest and our values conflict, what wins?*
- *Why is it so hard to change a habit?*
- *Do we sometimes think that a problem is so big that our action won't make an impact? So why bother?*

This conversation brings the team to Do the Math—the second step toward earning the Sage Award. Keep the "guilty habits" list because girls will check back with it later in the journey to see if they can cross anything off!

Do the Math!

A. CHOOSING AN ACTION

Girls will commit to lightening their own step on the planet by choosing two actions they will take to change a "bad" habit or start a new one. They will think creatively about how they can use math to visualize their impact. As they build toward their presentation on justice, they will think about how they can get other people "doing the math, too"—so they can make an even bigger impact.

Start by asking the girls to look back at the "Guilty Habits" collage and engage in some positive "What Ifs": *What if I adjust my habit of X, and then get my whole school trying to do the same? What if everyone at school also got their families involved?*

These footprint-reducing commitments can be things entirely within their personal control, such as a choice to not drink bottled water. Or, they could be something that would involve getting a group to make changes, such as a drive to recycle batteries in their neighborhood or compost food waste at their school. The girls can make a commitment as a team, too. There's no limit to doing the math!

Girls who choose the same challenge may want to compare notes with one another, and girls who choose different challenges will find it interesting to compare their results as well.

OPTION: WHAT IF?

The commitment to Do the Math is based on specific actions that can be easily measured. But suggest to girls that their commitments are also opportunities to do some blue-skies thinking that goes beyond conventional yardsticks. Invite to girls to take five minutes to ask some big What Ifs. What if everyone in the U.S. parked their car for a week? OK, that's not possible (or could it be? What would it take?!), but what if everyone drove 1,000 miles less each year? What would be the impact? Ask girls to speculate, and name six different possibilities.

What Ifs don't have to be serious. Challenge girls to come up with their own funny or outlandish What Ifs. It's a good chance to look at the world sideways, upside-down, and every which way. And who knows what good ideas might come from a What If!

As you wrap up, ask the girls: Why do leaders need an optimistic outlook? What innovations in the world are the result of an optimistic outlook? What do leaders and inventors probably have in common?

To encourage discussion, it might be helpful to pose questions like these:

- *Would it be best to commit to a challenge that is easiest to succeed at, or one in which the results can be largest or most noticed?*
- *What reasons might there be to pick the toughest challenge?*
- *What challenges would be easiest or hardest to get other on board with?*

TIP: Remind the girls that their considerations might be different for challenges they take on themselves and those they are trying to convince their family, school, or neighborhood to take on with them.

B. ENVISIONING AND MEASURING IMPACT

Usually, the more we see the impact of changes we make in our lives, the more likely we are to stick with our efforts and maybe even expand them and invite others to get on board, too. Here's where math comes in handy!

As girls pick their challenges, guide them to decide what yardstick they will use to visualize and measure their impact—it might be dollars, tons, or creative comparisons—and how they will record their progress. Some challenges will suggest specific yardsticks, but many will have several possibilities. Share the Do the Math examples on the next pages. They can check out examples in their book, too. If they don't come up with a Do the Math commitment right now, give them time to decide between gatherings. They might even discuss possibilities with a math or science teacher and ask for assistance in devising a creative way to show progress. Maybe the same teacher can even invite more students to join in on Doing the Math.

As the team's energy for Doing the Math takes off, you might suggest that girls start thinking about how these ideas and examples can assist them in making a powerful presentation on justice. What does math say and convey that could inspire change? What's the role of math as a communication strategy to get people moving?

HEALTHY PROTEIN RECIPE SWAP

It's great for people and Earth when we mix up our protein sources and don't over rely on one. You might ask the girls: *How about trying a new protein for one meal this week?*

Encourage them to go beyond cheese pizza and try dishes that might (or might not!) be new to them, like falafel with cucumber yogurt sauce, stuffed peppers with feta cheese, and rice or Indian curry with *paneer.*

Invite them to write their favorite new protein recipe on an index card and make enough copies for their teammates. At the next gathering, they can talk about how their meatless meal went over with their families and whether they might make it a weekly routine. Ask them: How does it feels to do something new that also is good for the environment? Then they can exchange recipe cards and cooking tips!

C. COMMITMENT CIRCLE

Let the girls know that by making a commitment to track the environmental consequences of their actions, they are measuring the impact, the footprint, of their daily decisions (and tying them to their values).

When we formally commit to a specific course of action, we are more likely to see it through than if we just think about a lot of different possibilities. So when the girls are ready, they can each write a specific commitment about what they promise to do, or write a team commitment together.

Get ideas from the team about how they would like to record and visualize the commitment: Jot it in their books? On the back side of the "guilty habits" list? Keep them on slips of paper in a team jar? Another way? What matters is capturing the commitments in such a way that the team can refer back to them as they track progress. Seeing progress encourages more progress!

Note that if the girls are not ready to commit to a specific behavior change today, they can keep thinking about it and regroup their Commitment Circle at the next gathering.

Do the MATH

What It Really Looks Like

BOTTLED WATER Do you drink bottled water? Did you know that every gallon of bottled water requires 3 gallons of water just to make the plastic bottle? If you've been drinking one bottle of water every day, how much money and water could you save by drinking tap water instead? And what if you could get three other people to pledge to stop drinking bottled water? And what if those three people each got three other people to stop? And what if those nine people each got three more people to stop? How much would all 40 of you save in a year?

Your Annual Consumption*

16 fluid ounces of water per day = 1/8th of a gallon (12.5% of a gallon)

12.5% gallon x 365 days = 45.625 gallons

45.625 gallons x 3 (gallons used to make plastic bottles) = 136.875 gallons of water per year for bottles

$1 (average cost of a 16–ounce bottle of water) x 365 days = $365

1 plastic bottle x 365 days = 365 bottles

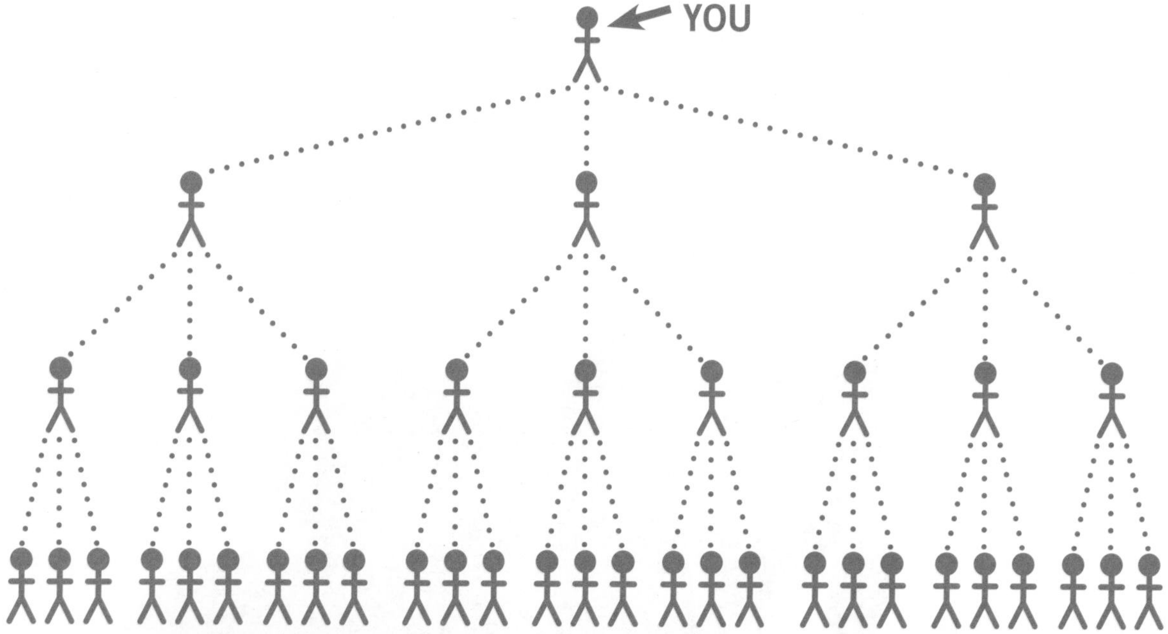

People	Gallons of water	$	Bottles
1	136.875	365	365
3			
9			
27			
Total: 40			

*Just pretend you drink one 16–ounce bottle of water per day

Do the MATH

COMPUTER/ COPY PAPER

How much computer/ copy paper does your school (or maybe the whole school system, if you're ambitious!) use in a month, and a year?

Using 1 ton (40 cases) of 30% post-consumer waste copy paper saves the equivalent of:

- 7.2 trees
- 2,100 gallons of water
- 1,230 kilowatt hours of electricity

Using 1 ton of 100% post-consumer waste copy paper saves the equivalent of:

- 24 trees
- 17 million BTUs of energy
- 2,108 pounds of carbon
- 8,750 gallons of water
- 1,124 pounds of garbage

Find out what sort of copy/computer paper your schools uses and then Do the Math. The next step? Advocate for change!

PAPER CUPS

Each year in North America, 130 billion paper cups are used! The production of these disposable paper cups consumes 50 million trees and 33 billion gallons of water. How many trees could you save if you stopped using paper cups? What if you asked three friends to also stop using paper cups and they each asked three friends? By yourself, you'd save more than one-tenth of a tree. All 13 of you would save a whole tree and a half! Just by doing nothing—by not using paper cups—you could save a tree!

ALUMINUM CANS

How many aluminum cans does your family (or school) recycle each week? Do the Math!

Recycling one aluminum can saves enough energy to run a laptop computer for 4 hours or a TV set for 3 hours. How much screen time can your family (or school) generate with the cans you recycle in a week, month, year?

Or you might build a commercial airline instead. If Californians recycled all the aluminum cans they buy in one day, they'd have enough aluminum to make 17 Boeing 727 jets. Calculate, based on the population of California and the population of your town, how long it would take your city to recycle enough to build a 727!

GO ALL OUT!

If girls are really interested in surveying to find out where people stand on environmental justice, or what they are willing to do to achieve it, they might want to add a whole session or two to the journey. Perhaps they even want to organize a field trip to survey people at a specific location (like a shopping mall or movie theater) or get expert advice on survey techniques from a local university or public opinion organization.

Surveying for More Perspectives

Offer a brief recap of the team's exploration of justice so far and introduce the idea of surveying others. You might say:

- *We've thought about how our values, visions, and habits contribute to or take away from justice.*
- *We've also thought a lot about the importance of "sitting at every stone" to grasp the big picture of environmental justice issues.*
- *We tried creating and ranking a list of issues that matter to us and saw that there is no such thing as a "simple list!" We've also examined case studies.*
- *Another way to get at what issues matter most, and what people are willing (or not!) to do about them, is to do a survey.*
- *Surveys are a great tool for understanding what others think. Of course there are many kinds of surveys and various ways to conduct them. As part of this journey, we'll experiment with a simple survey.*
- *It will give us a peek into the beliefs, the worries, and even the dreams of other people. That's valuable information for your equation for justice!*

Next, lay out the "simple list" from the first session, the "guilty habits" list from earlier today, and any commitments girls have made.

Ask: *So now, thinking about everything that you have done and explored so far, what do you want to learn from other people that would help you create an equation for justice?*

Here are some prompts you might offer as the girls decide on questions and create a survey:

- *Maybe you want to understand what people know about environmental issues and which are most important to them?*
- *Do you want to explore the "guilty habits" that people can't seem to stop, and what it is that stops them?*
- *Perhaps you want ideas about local environmental issues that worry people in this area and what they think should be done about them.*
- *Do you want to focus on a certain group of people—students, working people, parents . . . ?*

WRITING THE SURVEY

Guide girls to write up questions for a simple survey based on what they would like to learn from others at this point. Unless they are really planning to go all out, encourage them to keep it brief (5–10 questions will do) and focused. Review the "Survey Writing: Tips and Examples" handout on the next page of your guide will help them.

They will likely have one or two purposes for their survey: to learn what environmental issues people are concerned about and/or to find out what they are doing about those concerns. Here's a simple example of some questions girls might be interested in asking:

Have you ever tried to change a personal habit or routine in order to improve or protect the environment? What was it? Was it easy or hard? Have you continued? If not, why and what might you do different?

PLANNING TO CONDUCT THE SURVEY

Next, guide the Ambassadors to plan how and when they will conduct their survey. Will they use an online survey tool like Survey Monkey, or will they conduct their surveys in person? Will they survey people during the school day—say, at lunchtime? Or will they do it on a weekend at a mall or in a neighborhood park? Suggest that the girls estimate how much time they will need to conduct the survey. In some cases, it might take five minutes for girls to introduce themselves, explain the survey, and have the person complete the survey. But in other cases, girls may find that they can gather two or three people together to fill out surveys at the same time.

If each Ambassador can commit to surveying a few people between gatherings, *voilà!* The team will have a mini treasure trove of perspectives to consider when they come back together.

TIP

Suggest to the girls that while they are surveying they can also start building a network of people who might be interested in coming to their declaration of justice. If girls are surveying folks in person, invite the people who fill out surveys to also provide their contact info so that they can be invited to a final presentation on justice later.

Survey Writing: Tips and Examples

The best way to get the knack for writing good survey questions is to just try it! And then try answering the questions yourself, or ask a friend to respond. See if the questions:

(1) give you the information you were looking for, and (2) are so clear that they won't be misunderstood.

Having a specific goal in mind will guide your survey questions. What are you most curious about? Stay focused on your purpose! Here are some more tips:

- KISS: Keep it short and simple!
- Use clear, direct language.
- Decide what question format will give you the best information: yes or no answers, multiple choice, or a ranking or rating response, such as strongly agree, somewhat agree, don't know, somewhat disagree, strongly disagree.
- Make the first few questions interesting, and pretty easy. You don't want people to give up before getting started!
- Include all relevant choices in the list of possible answers and always include "don't know" as an answer choice.
- Avoid emotional words or phrasing that gives away an answer you might want. Be neutral. People often want to please the person asking the questions by giving her the answer they think she wants!
- At the end of the survey, ask basic information about age and gender. Keep the age groups simple: under 25, 25–50, over 50. Professional pollsters get much nosier than this, but Ambassadors don't need to!

Questions that can be improved	These questions will get you more information
1) Do you recycle cans and bottles?	**1) In the past month, what materials have you recycled? (check all that apply)** **❑ bottles ❑ cans ❑ paper ❑ plastic ❑ other ❑ none**
2) Is global warming a serious problem?	**2) Will global warming have a serious impact on the world in your lifetime?** **❑ very likely ❑ somewhat likely ❑ don't know ❑ somewhat unlikely ❑ very unlikely**
3) Can poisons in the environment harm children?	**3) Rank the following environmental health threats to children in order, with 1 being the most serious.** **__ pesticides in food supply __ contamination in water __ poor air quality __ lead poisoning __ other (please specify) ________**

Add to the Equation

As the gathering winds down, encourage the girls to reflect on what they now want to add to their justice definitions and equations (page 64 in their book). Here are some ideas to get them talking:

- *What do self-interests have to do with justice?*
- *How do we move from doing what is convenient to what is just?*
- *How do we move ourselves to act even in the face of a problem that seems so large that it is hard to imagine having an impact?*
- *How does visualizing results help? How can math help?*
- *Why is it important to act yourself before asking others to act?*
- *Can we be "scolded" out of our guilty habits? What are the alternatives?*
- *What would an imaginative record of the all cans or bottles recycled, the tons of carbon not emitted, the barrels of oil not burned, or the power plants not built or landfills not dug look like?*

Closing: "1 + 1 + 1 = 6"

Invite the girls to check out the "wonky arithmetic" of Cathy Zoi on page TK of their book. Perhaps each Ambassador can express how she thinks 1+1+1 could = 6 (or more!) when people Do the Math together for the environment.

Looking Ahead to Session 4

At their next gathering, Ambassadors will look at how environmental issues are handled in news stories and advertising, and how they can sharpen their critical thinking when it comes to viewing media. Ask the girls to collect their examples of environmental news stories and green marketing, so they can discuss them at the next gathering. If this topic is of great interest to them, they might also consider the following options toward completing Step 3 to the Sage Award (Be HAWK-EYED):

- assembling clips from movies, news programs, TV shows, and commercials and holding a "Hawk-Eyed" gathering or slumber fest to view and discuss them
- arranging to visit a university that offers a course on media analysis or related topics and inquiring about sitting in or speaking to the professor
- interviewing journalists and discussing how they look for truth
- gathering at a library or book store to investigate what book jackets and newspaper and magazine racks and other displays "say" about the environment

SAMPLE SESSION 4
Be Hawk-Eyed

AT A GLANCE

Goal: Girls sharpen their critical eye for environmental issues as they learn to look beyond the hype and get the facts. They also consider how getting the facts can be a good strategy for conflict resolution in their own lives!

- **Opening Ceremony: Yearning for Justice**
- **Check the Math**
- **Survey Says . . . !**
- **Beyond the Hype**
- **Get Dramatic: Act It Out!**
- **Creative Option: Picturing a New Justice**
- **Add It In!**
- **Conflicted? Try Facts**
- **Closing Ceremony: Hawk-Eyed**
- **Looking Ahead to Session 5**

MATERIALS

- **Beyond the Hype:** Supplement the articles the girls have gathered by looking out for environmental issues covered in newspapers, magazines, online articles, or in advertising
- **Picturing a New Justice:** any desired art supplies

PREPARE AHEAD

Based on plans made at the last gathering, the Ambassadors might be planning a special "Hawk-Eyed" outing for this session. Or perhaps a guest, such as a journalist, a media studies or communications professor, or an advertising executive could attend this gathering to assist the girls in analyzing the impact the media have on environmental justice.

Opening Ceremony: Yearning for Justice

Check out the Nature Break on page 93 of the girls' book. It encourages girls to take a short observational walk in silence while looking out for signs of nature thriving despite difficult circumstances. Perhaps the girls would like to try this for a few minutes with a walk around their gathering place. Then they can reflect together on this question: *What does the will of nature to keep growing tell us about our search for justice?*

Check the Math

Engage the team members in a discussion about the Do the Math actions they are trying to incorporate into their lives. Are any girls avoiding bottled water? Changing eating habits to lower their footprint? Reducing their trash? Walking or riding bicycles sometimes instead of driving? Ask:

- *How hard has it been to change these habits?*
- *Does changing them make things more or less convenient? Why?*
- *What have you learned or experienced that might convince others to change, too?*
- *Can anyone now cross a "guilty habit" off the list?*

Encourage the team to have fun thinking about some clever Do the Math visuals to show how the changes they're making are "adding up" to an impact. How many more behaviors could they change to create more of an impact? Who can they start inviting to Do the Math with them?

Survey Says . . . !

Now that the girls have collected their survey responses, they can tabulate and analyze the results. Even if they have not surveyed extensively, they can still get a taste of how surveys can be useful for obtaining various perspectives on problems and their possible solutions. Just remind the girls that this is a basic survey exercise—they won't want to draw too many conclusions based on it!

As the girls share and discuss their survey responses, you might ask:

- *Did the questions produce the information you were looking for?*
- *What responses were ones you most expected?*
- *What responses were the most surprising?*
- *What seems to matter to the people you surveyed? What seems to get in the way of action?*
- *How do the survey responses contribute to your equation for justice? What will it take?*

Encourage the girls to think of ways they can use what they have learned, from both Doing the Math and surveying others in their equation for justice.

Beyond the Hype

Kick off the exploration of media and advertising with this bird fact from page 72 of the girls' book:

Parakeets, budgies, and macaws are all talented mimics. The real trick is to take in what's around you, form your own opinion, and speak it!

Ask the girls for examples of how they feel they are influenced (positively or negatively) by media and advertising. Then guide the group to analyze news and advertising related to the environment.

If the girls have already collected and brought in some news stories on environmental issues, they can begin sharing their observations. Or they can take some time now to look through the clips they've collected, surf the Web, watch movie or TV clips, etc.

Ask for a volunteer to begin the discussion and let other girls follow up with their own thoughts. Encourage the girls to compare notes and ask one another questions, too. Here are some discussion starters that might be helpful (the girls have others on page 71 of their book):

- *What categories do the news stories fit into best?*
- *What patterns do you see in terms of geography or type of threat?*
- *How are different people characterized in the article, such as scientists, politicians, advocates, and those folks most directly affected by or exposed to the environmental threat?*
- *How much of a bird's-eye view is really provided? What's missing? Has the reader been able to "sit at every stone"?*

KEEP CAREER GOALS IN MIND

Every time girls interact with adults, they can be thinking about all the many career options possible in the world. For example, if there are guests on tap to talk about media and advertising as it relates to the "justice equation," encourage the girls to also ask questions about careers in these fields, education requirements, and even internship possibilities.

- *What gender dynamics might be at play here? Who is the author? Who is interviewed? Who is the publisher or producer?*
- *What kind of expertise is used? Can we trust the experts?*
- *Is math used? How? Could it be used better?*
- *What can you learn about creating environmental justice from these articles?*

After everyone has had a chance to weigh in with her thoughts and comments, invite the girls to move on to their findings about green ads and green marketing campaigns.

- *Do the ads seem truthful?*
- *How would you try to confirm their facts?*
- *Do the ads encourage you to feel a certain way about an issue? How?*
- *What do they make you think about the company and its products?*
- *Are there techniques you think you can borrow from these ads to persuade other people to join your commitment to environmental justice?*

Get Dramatic: Act It Out!

Suggest that the girls test out what they've learned about media through some creative role-playing. Have the girls divide into two teams. One team will pretend it is a multinational corporation about to announce a new green product—a hybrid car, a compostable plastic bottle, biofuel made from old gum or fingernail clippings, or whatever the girls can dream up! The other team will pretend that it is a team of newspaper reporters, bloggers, or environmental and consumer activists. The scene will be the company's annual shareholders' meeting.

- Give each group 10 minutes to huddle and create an improvised script.
- When time's up, assemble the teams to face one another. First, the corporation announces its grand green scheme, with testimony from company scientists and financial analysts. Then the journalists, environmentalists, and consumer watchdogs go to it!

Time may not permit another round (or the girls might be too tired from their dramatic exertions), but at the end of the mock confrontation, ask the girls what they would keep in mind if they had to switch roles.

- *What did the company folks learn from the environmentalists and journalists and vice versa?*
- *How would it make them more effective next time around?*

SAGE TEA

The girls might like to try this simple recipe for sage tea, an ancient use of the herb that was recommended for sore throats, coughs, nervousness, upset stomachs and other ailments, and for improving memory.

Pour 1 cup of boiling water over 1 tablespoon of fresh sage leaves or 1–2 teaspoons of dried sage. Let steep for 3–5 minutes. Strain and add lemon and honey, if desired.

Creative Option: Picturing a New Justice

Check out the "Nest" suggestion on page 28 of the girls' book, which asks the Ambassadors to find inspirational quotes, poems, or song lyrics that ignite their vision for justice. If this is an Ambassador team that enjoys getting crafty, the girls might like to devote some time to creating collages of images that evoke the feelings of justice, injustice, or a blend. You might say:

- *The symbol of justice as a blindfolded female figure holding scales and a sword dates back to antiquity. If you could come up with your own image of environmental justice, what would it look like?*
- *Think of images you associate with environmental justice, and then draw, paint, or collage them.*

To get them inspired, you might ask:

- *Does your vision include a lantern or a book to symbolize wisdom? A globe or clasped hands to show that environmental issues transcend national boundaries?*
- *What colors predominate? Blue for clean water and clear skies, or white for polar bears and melting glaciers?*

If the girls have a video camera or camera and tape recorder, they might record their Ambassador teammates—or children, friends, teachers and other people—offering ideas about environmental justice, and then put together a video or slide show. They might even include a sound track of music or sounds from nature!

Add It In!

Give the team time to add their insights about media and advertising into their definition and equation for justice (page 71 in their book). Here are some ideas and questions to spur discussion and reflection. Offer the opportunity for girls to think silently or talk as a team—or do a little of each.

- We have access to tidal waves of information! How can it help or hinder justice?
- Media is celebrated as freedom of expression and as vital to democracy. At the same time, it is also scorned and ridiculed as trivial and biased. How could the power of media be best used in an equation for justice?
- What techniques do media makers use to grab our attention? Which could we use for justice? How?

- How does advertising impact our values? Are there times when ads tell us what to value?
- How do we know what is true, right, and important?

Conflicted? Try Facts

Encourage the girls to apply "getting past the hype" to some conflict resolution possibilities for their own lives. Start by reminding the girls about their earlier "sit at every stone" discussion (Session 2). Ask:

- *Has anyone had a chance to try that out as a conflict-resolution strategy? What have you learned? If you haven't tried it, look for an opportunity to try it out—or observe when someone else (a teacher or parent) might be trying it!*
- *Can you recall times when you were involved in a conflict in which not everyone had the facts straight? What happens when people rely on gossip or misinformation? How can that contribute to conflict? How do you get the facts? Then, how do you have a conversation about the facts?*

Close by encouraging the girls to look out for opportunities to seek out facts as a conflict resolution strategy in their relationships.

Closing Ceremony: Hawk-Eyed

Note this bird fact from page 70 of the girls' book:

> *If you could see as well as a red-tailed hawk, you'd be able to read a newspaper from 30 feet away.*

Invite each girl to share what she would do if that's how sharp her vision was. The ideas can be just for fun, or serious, depending on the mood of the team!

Looking Ahead to Session 5

To complete the next step toward the Sage Award, girls will interview a scientist to understand how experts interpret scientific findings that lack certainty. Ask the girls if they have ideas about who they could interview to accomplish this step and where they would like to do it. (Also see Prepare Ahead suggestions in Sample Session 5.)

Would they like to take a field trip? Invite a guest to a gathering? Accomplish this step on their own, between gatherings? Who are some local science experts? Or is there an expert in another region, state, or country who would agree to a phone conversation or online chat with the Ambassador team?

ENCOURAGE GIRLS TO CONSIDER A RANGE OF EXPERTS

- environmentalists working for the government or a nonprofit organization
- engineers working on systems or inventions for green buildings
- a writer or editor who covers science issues
- a professional from a lab or pharmaceutical or chemical company
- students or professors from a university
- meteorologists from local news organizations

Talking with women in various STEM fields and asking questions about what is exciting about them opens the door for girls to see how science, technology, engineering, and math contribute to a better world.

SAMPLE SESSION 5
Take the Scientific View

AT A GLANCE

Goal: Girls investigate the role of science and uncertainty in environmental justice issues by interviewing a scientist and by exploring how various "expert" opinions can intertwine when environmental justice is at stake. Ultimately, girls consider what science can and cannot do for the environment.

- **Opening Ceremony: Invent It!**
- **Interviews: Interpreting Scientific Results**
- **Whose Opinion Really Counts?**
- **Add It In!**
- **Option: Controversy Strikes! You're the Scientist**
- **Closing Ceremony: If I Were a Scientist . . .**
- **Looking Ahead to Session 6**

MATERIALS

- **Whose Opinion Really Counts:** six index cards
- Whatever else the girls need for their chosen activities

PREPARE AHEAD

Check in with the girls on their arrangements for interviewing a professional about interpreting scientific findings. Depending on who the girls tap, and their plans for conducting the interviews, the ideas in this sample session can be adjusted accordingly. If you have a science guest or two visiting, they might enjoy participating in or guiding the exercises offered in this session.

To assist the girls in preparing for the interviews, review with them the "Interview Tips" on page 8–9 of this guide, and the additional tips in this session plan. Also make use of the interactive exercises the girls can explore in the "Taking the Scientific View" section of their book. You and the girls can choose what works best to shape your upcoming gatherings.

Opening Ceremony: Invent It!

Environmental justice issues nearly always involve some use of technology. Lots of time, effort, and brain power go into dreaming up green technologies that can reduce waste, curb pollution, and conserve resources. Girls have read about some examples of green technology in their book, and they've probably learned more as they collected examples of green marketing.

Ask the Ambassadors some big, wide-open questions along these lines:

- *If you could dream up a green technology, what would it be?*
- *If you were an engineer or designer, how would you change the world?*
- *How would you reduce your footprint with innovation?*

Then, offer some categories in which girls could suggest green improvements. Some possibilities include:

- *a less wasteful way to package a product you consume*
- *more energy-efficient ways to get to school*
- *greener jeans—or shoes, or anything else you wear*
- *cars or buses that produce less pollution*
- *renewable sources of energy your school might use*

As each girl names her inventions, she can either build on earlier ideas or offer something entirely new. Remind the Ambassadors that they can be practical and specific or they can reach for the sky.

CAREERS IN STEM

As girls think about how the power of science, technology, engineering, and math can be harnessed for justice, don't forget to also engage them in thinking about their future options in these fields.

Get the girls talking with women in these fields and asking questions about what is exciting about working in them.

Open some windows for the girls to see that careers in STEM can give them many opportunities to improve the world!

Interviews: Interpreting Scientific Results

Scientific experts help us get to the bottom of many issues. The ultimate goal of science is to reveal facts and processes that can be tested—chemical or physical laws, for example, that predict the same result no matter how many times you run an experiment.

How scientists go about analyzing and interpreting evidence can be a model for all of us. But there are times when even the scientific experts don't have the final word. What science actually is, in the everyday sense of the word, is a very human process of observation and discovery—that means even scientists can't always resolve issues with certainty! On some issues, we may never get the last word. And yet we will still have to make the best decisions we can, based on what we do know.

So here's the challenge for girls as they interview scientists: ***to understand the role science can play in an equation for justice.***

Perhaps the girls have arranged to talk to a science teacher, a university student or professor, a professional at the public health department, or a doctor. It's great if the Ambassadors can arrange to speak with someone who can give scientific examples related to environmental issues. But if not, the important thing is for the girls to get a better sense, in general, of how to analyze, interpret, and use scientific information.

- The girls should let their experts know that they are investigating the role that science plays in the way people make and decisions that impact the environment.
- They might also say that their main interest is walking through an example of how a scientific finding can be interpreted in various ways and used to lead the way to justice.
- Depending on the fields of their experts, the girls might like to reference an issue addressed in their book, or one of the recent controversies listed in the optional exercise (page 71 of this guide).

Depending on the girls' interest and the experts identified, the team will likely think of many topics to discuss. Don't forget to encourage them to ask for some educational and career advice, too! Here are some sample questions the girls could ask their experts:

- *Can you describe a fairly recent finding in your field that could be interpreted in more then one way?*

- *What are some of the observations, reasonings, experiments, and analysis that went into the finding?*
- *What is certain? What is uncertain? What are the risks or benefits associated with various interpretations of the finding? Who would they impact and in what way?*
- *How do you sort out what is known (and with what degree of certainty) and what is unknown?*
- *How do you decide how to interpret a finding like this?*
- *What does it take to be an expert in your field? Who in your profession do you consider an expert? Why?*
- *What role do you think science plays in creating more justice for Earth and all its inhabitants?*

Whose Opinion Really Counts?

Have the girls split into six groups. The groups don't have to be equal in size and even just one girl in a group is OK.

Explain the issue: *A new coal-burning power plant is being built along the river. The technology is the latest clean-coal technology, which is much better than the old power plants, but the project is still controversial.*

Then explain that six main groups have lined up on various sides of the issue:

1. People who live in the area. They will be most affected by any pollution, noise, or increased rail traffic involved in bringing in the coal.

2. SunPower, a solar and wind power plant company. It says their plant offers a cleaner alternative and won't cause health problems. (Economists, though, say the power will cost more than the power produced by the coal plant.)

3. Scientists. Most health researchers say the clean-coal technology isn't likely to affect health, but several caution that it could and the risk isn't known for sure. There are also environmental scientists who have been measuring the impact of the plant on the river, as well as the impact of the plant's turbines on bird migration. The results are mixed.

4. Homeowners and businesses. The plant is serving the needs of an expanding town and people want cheap power. But some of these folks belong to group 1 as well.

5. Politicians. They want to do the right thing for the town but are also nervous about how voters—and potential opponents—might respond to their support of one plant over the other.

6. Labor. People in the town want more jobs, but some of these folks are also in group 1.

Hand out one index card to each group, with the number 1 written on the front of each card. Then ask them to vote on whether the coal power plant should be built, based on the interests of their group.

Based on the Ambassadors' votes, does the plant get built?

Then take the cards back and ask each group to take a new one, but this time the cards are numbered from 1 to 6, based on the various group described in the scenario. But the numbers are on the back of the cards, so the girls can't see them before they choose.

Have the girls vote again, basing their decision on the number they drew.

Does the plant get built?

Ask the girls if they want to shuffle the cards and play again.

Wrap up the exercise with a discussion about how power is distributed among experts and stakeholders in environmental issues. Below are some conversation starters. No need to cover all of them!

- *How can people who have true expertise on an issue contribute to bringing about just decisions? What needs to happen for their voices to be heard?*
- *What, if any, kind of power do different experts seem to have toward creating just solutions?*
- *How do you separate real experts from wannabes? What does it take to be a real expert?*
- *Is there any such thing as a purely objective decision based on scientific facts?*
- *What combination of school, training, experience, and confidence is required to make a just decision?*
- *In a room of experts, whose expertise and/or experience matters most?*
- *When experts disagree, whose opinions should guide the public and how?*

Add It In!

Continue the tradition of inviting girls to think about what they will now add to their definition of justice, their equation, and their presentation possibilities based on their effort to understand how science fits in (page 94 in their book).

Separating scientific from non-scientific issues in an environmental justice case is never simple or entirely clear-cut. But it does help girls see how other considerations enter into the equation of finding solutions that are just.

Here are some points the team might consider:

- *How do we balance science, government, costs, and competing issues in the search for justice?*
- *Where do emotions and values come into the equation?*
- *What happens when decisions are based primarily on scientific data?*
- *In what ways could that help or hinder the goals of environmental justice?*
- *What considerations would be most important in a decision if the science is uncertain, such as a potential health risk or threat?*
- *In a team of decision-makers, when should scientific expertise be more important than other kinds of expertise? Are there cases in which it should it be less important?*
- *How should other perspectives—such as cost, politics, public acceptance, or basic human needs—be balanced with science?*
- *Would society make different choices if we all had a better understanding of the science of environmental problems?*
- *In what ways would the environment be protected if science and technology were harnessed differently?*

Option: Controversy Strikes! You're the Scientist!

Here's an opportunity for the Ambassadors to attempt to lay out the scientific facts and uncertainties behind some current controversies related to environmental justice.

Invite the girls to discuss any or all of the recent environmental controversies listed on pages 70–71, or other issues that interest them from their books or current local news. If they become really interested in a particular issue, they might even go further by organizing additional gatherings to research and debate what is known with certainty, what is unknown, and what additional information might solve the controversy.

Let the girls know that pulling apart scientific facts is trickier than it sounds. It may be known, for example, that a certain chemical at a certain concentration causes cancer in mice. But that does not mean it is "known" in the same way that the same chemical causes cancer in humans, or at what concentration it causes disease.

Girls will find a simple chart, like the one below, handy as they discuss the controversies. They can draw it out on a large sheet of paper.

Sorting Out the "Facts"			
WHAT IS KNOWN		**WHAT IS UNKNOWN**	
very certain	**fairly certain**	**very uncertain**	**fairly uncertain**

Scientific Information Needed to Raise the Level of Certainty

Non-Scientific Issues		
Reasons for disagreement on the issue:	**Parties involved in the disagreement:**	**What must change to reach a solution:**

RECENT ENVIRONMENTAL CONTROVERSIES

Some 80,000 chemicals are used in industry, agriculture, and manufacturing, and new chemicals are produced every year. It is impossible for researchers to test them all. And even when they test chemicals for safety, they don't look at the risk of being exposed to various combinations of these chemicals. No matter where you live, there are chemicals you are exposed to that some people feel are potential risks. Here a few that have caused recent controversies:

- **Phthalates and Bisphenol A** are ingredients in common plastics. Phthalates are used to soften and add flexibility to plastics but are also found in other products. Bisphenol A is used in hard plastics such as baby bottles and is also used in the coatings on the inside of food and beverage cans. Some companies and countries are phasing out their use of the chemicals because of growing health concerns.

- **Thiomersal** is a mercury compound that has been used as a preservative in vaccines since the 1930s. U.S. health agencies as well as the World Health Organization believe the additive is safe, but many people believe that thiomersal can trigger autism in some children.
- **Recombinant Bovine Somatotropin (rBST)** is a genetically engineered growth hormone used to boost milk production in cows. But because the hormone is produced synthetically, people fear there may be hidden dangers that are not yet known. Consumer groups have lobbied the government to label milk produced from cows given rBST, and some grocery store chains have pledged not to sell the milk.
- **Genetically modified** foods are also the result of bioengineering, and they've been criticized, too. Supporters of the technology say it enables scientists to create more nutritious, higher-yielding varieties of crops. A type of genetically modified rice called golden rice contains higher amounts of vitamin A, which could prevent blindness in people with a common deficiency of that nutrient. Critics of genetically modified foods, however, call it "frankenfood." They warn that there may be unforeseen health and ecological consequences from what they consider unnatural plant varieties.

Closing Ceremony: If I Were a Scientist

If the girls don't have a special closing in mind, how about a "quick whip around," with each girl completing this sentence:

If I were a scientist, I'd contribute to environmental justice on Earth by

____.

Looking Ahead to Session 6

At the next gathering, the girls will put the decision-making process under their Ambassador microscope. They'll ask: *What's involved in making decisions and what makes some decisions especially difficult? Can we track the footprint of our decisions?* Engage the girls in brainstorming who they can interview about making decisions that impact the environment—and guide them to make plans accordingly. You may find it helpful to check the related information in Sample Session 6, beginning on page 72.

SAMPLE SESSION 6
Decipher Decisions

AT A GLANCE

Goal: Girls explore the complexity of decision-making when various needs compete. Ultimately, they develop ideas about "just decision-making" to add to their growing equations for justice.

- **Opening Ceremony: I Changed My Mind!**
- **Check the Math**
- **Interview a Decision-Maker**
- **Tracking the Footprint of a Decision**
- **Add It In!**
- **Closing Ceremony: The Best Decision I Ever Made**
- **Looking Ahead to Session 7**

MATERIALS

- Paper, pens, and pencils and anything else the girls need to prepare for their interviews

PREPARE AHEAD

As they progress toward the Sage Award, the girls will interview an adult (or several) involved in making a difficult decision related to environmental concerns. Notice the ideas given on page 104 of the girls' book.

The team can adapt the suggestions in this session plan according to how and when they conduct their interviews. Tips and ideas for the interviews are offered in "Interview a Decision-Maker."

Before the session, check in with the girls about who they can tap to explore decision-making with. Perhaps a contact from their school, place of worship, or neighborhood can assist? Who do the girls' parents and relatives know? What local zoning or land decisions have been made and featured in the local news recently? Can the team track down someone who has been involved?

Opening Ceremony: I Changed My Mind!

Invite girls to consider the question: *What have you changed your mind about lately?*

What the girls choose to talk about doesn't necessarily have to involve a decision, good or bad. But it is a great reminder that we do—and should—change our mind about things. That goes for organizations of all shapes and sizes, too.

Ask for a volunteer to start off by finishing this sentence:

I changed my mind about ____.

Then have each girl take a turn. They don't have to give any reason or explanation. And, in fact, it will be more fun and faster paced if they don't. Each girl's answer will, in turn, trigger ideas for other girls. The mind-changing declarations can be about food, music, clothes, people, whatever they have changed their mind about recently. The girls can go as many rounds as they like and can even announce the round's topics as they go.

Check the Math

How are the girls doing with their commitments to change a habit for the good of the environment? Does anyone have a nifty math equation, or a visual representation of Doing to Math to share? Check out the "guilty habits" list the girls created earlier. Can any get crossed off? You might ask: *What do our small everyday actions tell us about the big picture of environmental justice?*

Interview a Decision-Maker

The Ambassadors will interview adults who have had to make tough decisions. The girls will strive to walk in the shoes of those individuals in order to learn how they came to the decision they did. Each girl will try to determine:

- What made the decisions difficult?
- What was the process by which she arrived at her decision?
- What did she learn that she can apply to other situations in life?
- How does one make the best possible decision (what's the equation?)

Let the girls know that the goal of interviewing adults who have made tough decisions related to the environment is to understand how competing issues often come into play in decision-making. As they continue to think about their own equations for justice, what can the Ambassadors build into their equations so that they strive toward sound decision-making practices? No matter what the issue at hand might be, encourage the girls to learn as much as they can about "just decision-making" in general.

As girls brainstorm questions to ask their selected decision-makers, offer some assistance from the list of possible interview questions that starts below. The girls don't have to ask all the questions listed. And they'll likely have great ideas of their own to contribute.

Encourage the girls to think about how they could gain some new insights into educational and career possibilities while conducting the interviews. They might add in questions like: *What's an average day like for you? How did you become involved in this kind of work? What interests you about it?*

20 QUESTIONS

Playing a few rounds of a game like Twenty Questions or Animal, Vegetable, Mineral could be a fun and helpful warm-up for preparing for an interview. These guessing games about an object a person is thinking about are actually better described as "interview" games. It takes asking the right questions to get the right answers.

POSSIBLE INTERVIEW QUESTIONS

- *What decision were you most involved in making?*
- *What was your role?*
- *Who else was involved?*
- *How did the need to make this decision come about? What led up to it?*
- *What questions did the you ask yourself and how did you identify your priorities?*
- *Did you make lists?*
- *Whom did you ask for advice and what questions did you ask?*
- *What role did your personal values play and what values were most important to you as you moved toward a decision?*
- *How did your heart and head share the decision-making process?*
- *How did you use scientific information?*
- *Were you confident that you had the big picture of what was going on?*
- *Did you weigh various possible outcomes? How?*
- *Was your decision final, or was it one you could later revisit and revise?*
- *What has been the impact of your decision?*
- *What would you do differently next time?*

Decisions by Committee

Not all decisions are personal, of course, and the Ambassadors may want to focus instead on a decision made by an organization, such as a policy position taken by a city or state government agency, an environmental organization, a corporation, or a local advocacy group. In these cases, the girls will want to explore the additional elements that come into play when decisions are made by groups.

Here are a few suggestions for how to expand the scope of an interview to cover the decision-making process of an organization:

- *How many people were involved in the decision?*
- *Was it a group decision by vote, or did the decision follow some sort of chain of responsibility?*
- *If so, could this chain of responsibility, or decision tree, be graphically represented?*
- *How did the team divide up responsibilities?*

HERB SAMPLING PARTY

Herbs can add great flavor to vegetables, beans, grains, and other protein-rich alternatives to meat. Let the girls get familiar with their fabulous flavors during an herb taste test! They might even want to try it blindfolded—just like the image of Justice balancing her scales!

Gather a sampling of common herbs, such as basil, mint, chives, tarragon, dill, and parsley. And don't forget sage! Include a few less familiar herbs, too, such as lemon verbena, which has a refreshing lemon taste; chervil, which has a subtle, anise-like taste; and epazote, also known as Mexican tea or wormseed, which has a strong licorice flavor. Give the herbs a rough chop, and set them out. It might be nice to have on hand a mild soft cheese, such as cream cheese, and crackers.

Have the girls sample the herbs one by one. Encourage them to sniff them and to compare their colors and textures. Ask: *What does the taste remind you of? Are there certain dishes you're familiar with that use these herbs? Do any of the herbs taste like licorice or onion or lemon? What dishes might you use the various herbs in? Does anyone know if any of the herbs are reputed to have medicinal qualities?*

- *Were experts involved and what role did their experience play in the decision?*
- *Did ultimate responsibility for the decision fall on one person?*
- *Who or what would the decision have an impact on, and how would that impact be measured?*

Tracking the Footprint of a Decision

An important element in examining decisions, whether made by individuals or by organizations, is to see how a decision impacts future decisions. Encourage girls to consider a decision's larger footprint. They can select an issue or a case described in their books, the decision discussed during their interviews, or another local issue they have become aware of while on this journey. Here are some questions to guide the conversation.

- *Once a decision is made, in what ways could it narrow future decisions?*
- *How might a different decision broaden the field of future decisions?*
- *In what ways could these considerations be used in the decision-making process to arrive at better decisions?*

Suggest to Ambassadors that they include a "bad decision" in their scrutiny of decisions, or at least one that had bad consequences. This is certainly the case in many instances of environmental justice, where decisions often prove to have unforeseen and regrettable consequences.

They might call this "Tracking the Footprints of an Abominable Decision."

- *How did it become apparent that the decision was bad? Who or what determined—and how—that it was bad? Was it someone's job to follow the footprint of the decision?*
- *Was it obvious right away, or did it take time, consequences, and other decisions to make it clear that the original decision led down the wrong path?*
- *What was done once it became clear that it was the wrong decision or that the decision had to be revised or corrected by another decision?*
- *Is reversing or changing a decision different than making a decision?*
- *If so, what other considerations are included in the decision-making process?*
- *Should the team or individuals involved in making the original decision be included in revising that decision? If so, how?*

ONE GIRL'S TRASH...

. . . is another girl's treasure.

It's true! Probably that shirt you now hate, the bracelet you're sick of, or the shoes that just don't do it would be the perfect thing—for someone else!

Reduce your waste (not to mention clear your clutter and free up some mind space for justice) by organizing a swap with your friends. Better yet, get their friends and families in on it, too! (Yes, it's still all about math!) Maybe you can score a book you actually need, a "new" bag, or even a lovely "old" bike.

Add It In!

Invite the girls to add to their equation (page xx in their book). You might ask:

- *What will you add into your equation for justice about decision-making?*
- *What's are the "top 5" things to do when making a decision so that it turns out to be a good one?*
- *What are the "top 5" things to avoid doing when making a decision?*

Closing Ceremony: The Best Decision I Ever Made

Perhaps the Ambassadors would like to close on a personal note, each sharing a great decision they have made in their lives! Where has the footprint of the decision led them?

Looking Ahead to Session 7

In Session 7, girls will be putting together their definition of justice and their equation for what it will take to create it. Girls can do this as a team, as mini-teams, or as individuals. They will bring together all the elements in a presentation that will define what they have learned about the journey to justice and what they want most to communicate to an audience of their choosing. Encourage girls to bring all their insights, notes, team collages, etc. to the next gathering!

TIE IT TO CONFLICTS!

Look for opportunities to encourage girls to link their thinking about what it takes to create justice to strategies they could use to resolve conflicts in their own lives. For example, while girls tackle the complexities of decision-making, they can talk about:

- When does it help to try bringing a conflict to a neutral decision-maker?
- Who could that person be?
- What would she need to know to help resolve the conflict?

SAMPLE SESSION 7

What's the Equation?

AT A GLANCE

Goal: Girls access "add it in" notes and ideas they've made along the journey, create their definition and equation for justice, and choose the audience for their presentation. They also consider some "new equations" for themselves as they talk about what they have learned about career options along their journey.

- **Opening Ceremony: Toward Justice Once Again**
- **Career Equations**
- **The Equation: Add Up All the Insights**
- **Who Cares?**
- **Reaching Out**
- **Closing Ceremony: Hope and Despair**

MATERIALS

- **The Equation:** Any team lists, collages, or other 'tools" that have been developed along the journey ("Toward Justice," "A Simple List," "Guilty Habits," etc.); paper, pens, a computer; other supplies needed for any creative endeavor the girls choose to help capture and reflect their definition and equation for justice

PREPARE AHEAD

Think back over all the steps along the journey and all that the girls have explored. Be ready to coach them to combine all their insights into a new equation for justice!

Opening Ceremony: Toward Justice Once Again

Gather the team around the "Toward Justice" sheet they made during the first gathering of the journey. Invite the girls to consider the questions and ideas they captured at that time and to think about what they've learned about creating justice since then. You might ask:

- *What are you more aware of now than you were earlier on?*
- *What has surprised you? What makes you feel hopeful?*
- *Does anything make you feel sad?*

Then ask each Ambassador to fill in this statement:

One thing I would like everyone to know about justice for Earth is

____.

The team might want to jot these down on a new collage that they can then use to shape their equation and upcoming presentation.

Career Equations

Encourage the girls to take a time out from planning their "justice equation" to think and talk about the ideas this journey has given them for the future.

Start by inviting the girls to flip through their book to check out all the stories about what women are doing around the world for justice. Also remind the girls of the people they've have met and talked to on this journey.

Suggest that each girl choose one career she never thought of before and spend a few minutes thinking about what it would be like to work in this field. To get the girls started, offer a few questions, like these:

- *What would you need to study for this career?*
- *What would be most exciting about this career?*

- *What would be most challenging?*
- *What would you hope to accomplish in this career?*
- *Whose help would you need to be successful in this career?*
- *Who do you already have in your network who might assist you?*
- *How can you meet other people in this field?*

After the girls have had time to think about possible career paths, invite them to trade their ideas with one another.

Wrap up with a discussion centered on this question: *Why is it important to be open to the many career possibilities in the world?*

Then encourage each girl to make a commitment to "cultivate career curiosity," especially as she reads the news, surfs the Web, or talks to adults in her growing network. Remind the team: *Life is one big career exploration, and it's full of opportunity!*

The Equation: Add Up All the Insights

No matter how creative the girls plan to be in presenting their equation for justice, they'll find it helpful to begin by outlining the basic points of their equation. Engage them in pulling their big ideas together, using key points from all their gatherings along the journey.

Encourage the girls to think about how they could incorporate any of the journey "tools" they've already created, such as the justice questions and visions from Session 1, and their "guilty habits" list and Do the Math items.

Below begins a step-by-step summary of the explorations the Ambassadors took part in throughout *JUSTICE*. Use it to offer some thought starters to the girls if they're not sure how to begin. As always, adjust the ideas and examples given as needed, based on the team's energy and thinking. Who knows? At this point, the Ambassadors may already be off and running with their own well-thought out plan!

JUSTICE: A BIG-PICTURE SUMMARY

Look High, Look Wide: *Why is a bird's-eye view important for justice? What happens when you forget to "sit at every stone?" What's possible when you get a great big perspective?*

Do the Math: *What happens when self-interests and environmental concerns collide? How can you choose to act? What does it take to make an impact?*

How does Doing the Math help? What "guilty habits" have we overcome? What would it take for other people to overcome some, too?

Be Hawk-Eyed: *How do the media and advertising inform our decisions and habits related to the environment? How could the power of the media and advertising be harnessed for justice?*

Take the Scientific View: *How can science create justice? What are its limits?*

Decipher Decisions: *How do you make a just decision? How do you reverse an unjust one? What is required to make a just decision?*

To pull their main ideas together, encourage the girls to jot some key thoughts on large pieces of paper. They might start with this template:

First, Define It! Justice for Earth and all her inhabitants =

Now, Build the Equation! You reach this vision of justice by

- Adding ________________ to __________________
- Subtracting _______________ and _______________
- Multiplying by the total by ______________________

Creating a series of "top" lists is another good way for the girls to organize their thinking. They could list their "Top 5" steps toward justice and their "Top 5" things to avoid when seeking justice.

Who Cares?

With a basic definition and equation for justice mapped out, the girls can now decide whom they want to share it with. They can then plan their presentation, based on their invited audience and the kind of gathering they envision.

Guide the team to identify their audience by asking questions like these:

- *Who could benefit from learning about what it takes to create justice?*
- *Whom have you met and spoken to along the journey who will be interested in hearing the end result of your thinking?*
- *Who is involved in making local decisions and could perhaps gain some fresh perspective from your insights?*
- *What environmental and civic groups would be interested in hearing some of the examples and ideas?*

POPCORN AND THE PRESS

Like detectives and secret agents, journalists make good movie characters. It's exciting watching reporters run down leads, get scoops, race to meet deadlines, and wrestle with moral and ethical dilemmas. It can also be instructive.

How about watching a movie that deals with journalists and the media, and then discussing the issues it raises? Movies to consider include "Mr. Smith Goes to Washington," "All the President's Men," "The Killing Fields," "Broadcast News," "The Insider," "Shattered Glass," "Good Night and Good Luck," and "The Devil Wears Prada."

You might ask the girls: *What ethical issues did the movie raise? How did the characters deal with them? What scene made the strongest impression on you? What was said or shown that gave the scene its punch? Did it touch your emotions or intellect or both? Is there a way to use those techniques in your JUSTICE presentation?*

If the group doesn't have a nose for news, how about a movie night filled with heroines striving toward justice? Seek out films with eloquent speeches or images of nature that appeal to our hearts and minds!

- *Who could you inspire to change, even just a little? Who needs a jolt of optimism?*
- *Who could you share your Do the Math commitment with?*
- *What teachers or counselors or clubs at school might be interested?*
- *Do you know people at local places of worship who might find your message inspiring?*
- *How about elected officials or their staff members? Town, school, or library board members?*

Reaching Out

As the girls create a list of potential participants, they can turn their attention to how to plan an event, or several small events, to showcase their presentation. Based on their list, what makes sense—one large gathering or several small ones? Can there be an interactive display station or gallery that will remain in place after the presentation? Do the girls envision working with a small group of people—a roundtable conversation? A larger group? Maybe there are already meetings taking place in school, the community, a place of worship, a library, or town hall that girls could tap into, instead of hosting a separate gathering. These questions will aid the girls in their planning.

- *What ideas and interests will your anticipated audience contribute to gathering? Will they want to talk and interact or mostly listen?*
- *What is your goal in inviting the people you've identified?*
- *How will you motivate them to attend?*
- *What's the most effective way to invite these people? Which people will you have to call, who will you e-mail, and who can you ask in person?*
- *How much notice will be enough?*
- *What advantages might there be to getting ourselves on the agenda of some other event or meeting going on instead of planning our own?*

Closing Ceremony: Hope and Despair

The girls may have their own idea for ending today's gathering. If not, sharing their opinions on these questions will make an interesting closing reflection:

- *When is it important to show and discuss "injustice?" And when is it important to show the hope of justice?*
- *How do the two best work together to compel us to act?*

SAMPLE SESSION 8

Who Will Listen?

AT A GLANCE

Goal: Girls continue to plan their presentation to define justice and share an equation for achieving it.

- **Opening Ceremony: Inspiration, Please!**
- **Presentation Preparations**
- **Conflicted? Listen More!**
- **Celebration Planning**
- **Closing Ceremony: Check the Math**

MATERIALS

- Plans and summaries from last gathering.
- Creative supplies as needed.

PREPARE AHEAD

A great potential guest for this session would be a public relations professional. Do the girls or their families know anyone who gives speeches on behalf of a local cause or organization? How about a community relations representative for a company or someone from a news or advertising agency?

This person could share tips with the girls as they pull their presentation plans together. And remember: Any time girls meet someone new, it's a chance for them to discuss new ideas about college and career possibilities!

Opening Ceremony: Inspiration, Please!

If girls haven't done so yet, they might like to flip through the examples of women around the globe featured in their book. Then each could describe how and why one of the women inspires them. Have they uncovered local women striving for justice? Now's a good time to tell those stories, too!

OPTION: IF YOU CAN SEE IT . . .

Coaches encourage elite athletes to do it, and doctors suggest that patients practice it, too. It's visualization: seeing in your mind's eye the winning finish of a race, the successful execution of a complicated dive or gymnastics vault, or the healing process that returns a person to health. Meditating on the sequence of steps that will carry a person to her goal is great reinforcement for making that goal a reality.

Ask for a volunteer to suggest a case study of injustice—one the team has become aware of locally or one from the girls' book. Then invite the girls to imagine each of the steps needed to arrive at a better solution—and justice. Encourage them to think of the steps they have explored in their journey, from taking a broader perspective and analyzing the facts to understanding the roles of various parties in the decision-making process.

Invite the Ambassadors to suggest other case studies. In what instances are the steps the same or different and why? Visualizing the solution to a problem can be a good way for girls to test their equations for justice. It is also a terrific way to cultivate optimism!

Presentation Preparations

Continue coaching and encouraging the team to pull together their justice definition and equation and a plan for sharing it with the designated audience. Ask girls to check that they have:

- a clear definition of justice that they believe in and are eager to share
- an equation for how we can get more justice going on Earth
- examples of how we can all strive toward justice in our daily lives
- an invitation to join the Ambassadors in Doing the Math

Girls can also use this session to divvy up and practice their speaking points, design and create visuals, put photos or video clips together, etc. Coach the team so that each girl has an opportunity to contribute some of her unique skills and talents to the creative aspects of the presentation.

Also, confirm plans to ensure that the identified "audience" will indeed show up at the planned event. Nothing's worse than being all set to present and finding out that the seats are empty! What steps need to happen to ensure that the Ambassadors' efforts will have an audience?

TIPS FOR GREAT PRESENTATIONS

Ambassadors will have had experience making class presentations or addressing groups. But no matter how expert they are, most presenters find it helpful to be reminded of what makes a great presentation. Encourage girls to check out the tips on pages 108–111 of their books. And offer the following additional ones—along with any of your own.

Do You Open with a Bang? That can be great, but don't worry too much about it if your material doesn't include one. Do find an opening that is compelling and engages your audience right away. It might be dramatic photos, statistics, or a story that best captures your message.

Confidence Matters: Nearly everyone feels a bit nervous when they are in the spotlight. But the more you focus on the audience—who they are, why they are here, and what you want to tell them—the less you focus on yourself. Knowing your message goes a long way in calming butterflies. Having a couple of familiar, friendly faces in the audience helps, too.

Know Your Presentation Style and Strengths: Are you comfortable working from notes or will you want much of it written out? If it's the latter, you'll need to build in spots where you look up, click on a slide, or show a photo. Reading from a full script is probably a last resort. But memorizing it is almost always a bad idea, too. At most, memorize your opening and closing. Index cards can sometimes be a happy medium. Don't know your presentation style? Try each to see what you are most comfortable with.

Consider Signposts: This is a technique that presentation coaches often suggest as a way to help your audience follow and remember what you're saying. Examples of phrases that help focus listening are: "The most important thing to remember is . . . " or "What many people don't realize is . . . " Another strategy is to number your points, "My first (and second and third) point is . . . " or "I'd like to leave you with two main ideas . . . "

Offer Handouts: Some presenters will give audiences an outline of their talk, with key points, before they begin. That can be helpful, but only if the outline is short. You don't want your audience reading instead of listening. The time to hand out more extensive printed materials is at the end of your presentation, but tell the audience early in your talk that this is what you plan to do. That encourages people to sit back, relax, and listen.

Mind Your Body Language: We all know that we communicate with our bodies, but it's still so easy to let nerves get the best of us. Remind girls of the old standbys: make eye contact, keep your head up, shoulders down and relaxed, use your hands if it feels natural, and don't stand perfectly still, but don't wander. Ask the girls to think of the worst body-language mistakes they've made or seen made by other speakers. No names, mistakes only!

Practice, Practice, Practice: Everyone has her own ideas about how to practice a speech or presentation. Invite the girls to share theirs. Who talks to a mirror? Who rehearses with family, friends, and other Ambassadors?

How Will You Involve Your Audience? One way to engage the audience, which is mentioned in the girls' book, is to offer a case study for them to work with. Girls can also consider questions they might ask their audience. Show-of-hands questions are usually the best, along the lines of: "How many people have ever noticed . . . " or "Who has seen a . . . " They involve the audience but don't interrupt the flow of your presentation.

COVER ART AS INSPIRATION

Suggest this creative boost to the girls as they consider how to present their equation:

Encourage them to check out the cover treatment on their book. Do they notice how the cutout letters of *JUSTICE* actually reveal images of injustice?

What local examples can the girls think of?

- A beautiful beach, park, lake, or mountain with trash strewn about?
- A lovely pair of ducklings swimming through a trash-filled pond!
- A little shrub sprouting in an untended lot?

How can girls capture and make use of images such as these to inspire others with the double message of the beauty (and justice!) possible on Earth *and* the reality of the work ahead of us all?

Wrapping It Up: Audiences remember closings, so make yours memorable. It doesn't have to be complicated. And consider marking it with a signpost, something like: "I hope you found my presentation interesting and hope it will get you thinking about what we can all do to support environmental justice."

Follow Through and Follow Up: Offer resources where your audience can get more information and invite people to contact you with comments or questions. A handout they can return to you is an easy way to encourage this.

Conflicted? Listen More!

Engage the girls in a short re-cap of the ways in which thinking about the big picture of justice has contributed to bettering their strategies for resolving conflict in their lives. For example, how can "sitting at every stone" help? Getting the facts? Seeking a neutral decision-maker? Which of these have they tried to do more often? What have they learned?

What other parts of their "equation for justice" have they noticed that relate to better conflict resolution in relationships?

After a good discussion, ask the girls about the "art of listening":

- *When is it hard to listen to others? Why?*
- *When is listening an important strategy to use to resolve conflicts?*
- *When do they wish others would listen to them more?*
- *How might they ask for this?*

Depending on time and interest, the girls might like to capture their top strategies for resolving conflicts in an "Ambassadors' Advice" tip list and make plans to educate and inspire younger girls by sharing the list with them.

Celebration Planning

Before the session ends, get a brainstorm going about how girls would like to end their journey in search of justice. Do they envision . . .

- an outing or party just for the team?
- a more formal gathering to receive their Sage Awards?
- linking up with other Ambassador groups in the area?
- an opportunity to inspire younger Girl Scouts?

- time away enjoying nature?
- a little of each?

Share with the girls the "Celebrate" ideas offered in Session 10, too. Based on their preferences, encourage the Ambassadors to start planning their closing gathering:

- They might think about all the people they have spoken to and gotten assistance from along the way. Will they make thank-you calls or send notes? Perhaps a newspaper or radio station will help them acknowledge the support.
- Ask the girls to revisit the information about the Sage Award and the meaning of "sage" on page 10 of their book. What kind of award ceremony would they like to design for themselves as they gift each other with the award?
- As girls think about all they have accomplished together, they might also like to think about the ways in which they have acted sagely as a team and as individuals. Would they like to choose a name and plan little awards for one another based on personal qualities and skills shared with the team? Who came through with interview connections? Who shared sage snacks? Who reminded us why we love the outdoors?

Based on their ideas, resources, and time available, guide the team members to divvy up tasks and plan their closing celebration together.

Closing Ceremony: Check the Math

Gather the team and get out the "guilty habits" list from Session 3. Ask:

- *What guilty habits could you now cross off?*
- *How does crossing items off make you feel? Round of applause, anyone?*
- *What creative math can you show to demonstrate your impact?*
- *Are there items remaining on the list that are harder to cross off? Which? Why?*
- *What next? What Do the Math items might you like to add into your presentation plans?*

SAMPLE SESSION 9
Inspiring Justice

AT A GLANCE

Goal: Girls share their vision of justice—what it means and how we get it—with others and invite everyone to make strides toward justice by Doing the Math. Following their presentation, girls take time to talk through everything they've explored along the journey.

- **Coaching Tips**
- **Feeling Sage?**
- **Next Steps and Celebration Planning**

MATERIALS

- Any visuals or other materials needed for the girls' presentation

PREPARE AHEAD

Engage the girls in double- and triple-checking their presentation plans, materials, and invited audience. Depending on the logistics of the gathering and time available, you and the girls can enjoy the "Feeling Sage?" activity either after the presentation, at a gathering you plan especially for this debriefing, or as part of a special closing celebration of the journey.

Coaching Tips

All may not go as planned. Life usually does not! Provide Ambassadors with plenty of encouragement related to any hiccups they experience. Not everyone came? Follow up with photos and presentation highlights to share the news anyway. Can a display station be maintained? Presentation equipment failed? A speaking point was missed? We forgot to bring commitment cards to capture the Do the Math promises? Encourage the girls to improvise, adjust, and look at what they learned that will serve them well on some other journey in life.

Feeling Sage?

Don't let the journey end without an "ambassadorly" talk about all the girls have learned and experienced. This is a chance to touch back on both the personal commitments and "justice insights" the girls have realized along the way. Consider these points to round out the discussion:

Your Equation

- *How did it feel to share it with others?*
- *What do you think you got your audience thinking about?*
- *How will you keep using your equation—and adding to it?*

Toward Justice

- *Remember that team collage of ideas, ideals, and questions we started at our first gathering?*
- *What new or different ideas do you have now? What questions?*
- *How might you make a commitment to keep exploring?*

Guilty Habits and Doing the Math

- *What personal habit have you changed along the way?*
- *What have you learned by trying to change it?*

Conflicts in our Own Lives

- *What new strategies are you using?*
- *What works?*

Career Equations

- *What new insights do you have about your future?*
- *How will you continue to cultivate your curiosity about what is possible?*

Nesting, Soaring, and Nature BREAKS

- *What have you enjoyed about taking time to nest, soar, and enjoy nature?*
- *How do some of the things we've tried help you keep balance in your life?*

Next Steps and Celebration Planning

Firm up plans for the journey's closing, based on the girls' ideas. Remind girls about finding ways to thank everyone who has supported them along the way.

Also, check in about any new ideas that emerge as a result of the presentation. Do girls want to continue any of their efforts in some way? Follow up with participants who have committed to doing the math?

Ask girls what they think is feasible and what they may be interested in doing now that they have shared their vision of justice with others.

Remind the team too that there are many ways for them to continue being involved in Girl Scouts. Perhaps they can check in with their Girl Scout council for opportunities related to camp, special events, travel, or even assisting with younger girls!

If girls have identified local issues along this journey and want to advocate for change, now would be a great time for them to embark on a *Your Voice, Your World* journey. And if they've already done that, they might consider going after their Girl Scout Gold Award! They can check out the requirements at www.girlscouts.org.

SAMPLE SESSION 10
Celebrate!

AT A GLANCE

Goal: The girls reflect on what they have learned along their journey toward justice, enjoy a closing celebration, and take a look at how they might continue their pursuit of justice.

- **Celebrate**
- **Sage Award Ceremony**

MATERIALS

- Whatever the girls need for their celebratory closing

PREPARE AHEAD

This session offers a variety of options and ideas for girls to use to bring a celebratory end to their journey to justice. Share them all with the girls and encourage them to mix and match to create their very own sage ending to their adventure.

JUSTICE Celebration Options

Start a Flight Pattern for Justice

Keep the math going. You are a Girl Scout Ambassador. There are thousands more of you across the country— and if you add in your WAGGGS sisters around the world, you could get a whole lot of justice going.

What would you like to do to share equations for justice with girls across the country and around the world? You might consider closing your journey with some digital connections.

Fly Back

Do some more math. You have millions (truly!) of younger Girl Scout sisters. Start with the thousands in your own region, or even just the Ambassadors in your school district. What did you do along this *JUSTICE* journey that you can "pass on down" to inspire your younger sisters?

- *Can you share your equation so they can build on it?*
- *Perhaps your closing ceremony can be a way to hand off a call to justice to younger girls.*
- *If you're feeling crafty, how about a making a keepsake of some kind that contains your equation and invites incoming Ambassadors to add their own?*

JUSTICE Celebration Options

Up, Up, and Away

Talk to the people you have presented your equation to. What commitment did you ask them to make? Are they Doing the Math? If you've taken the *Your Voice, Your World* journey, can you find some evidence of "the butterfly effect" you may have started (big or small).

Celebrate by creating a poem, sketch, photo collage, or other expression that shows what happens when people come together to seek justice.

Nest

Perhaps you and your Ambassadors friends are ready for a team huddle, a chance to celebrate your accomplishments along this journey. You might emphasize personal accomplishments—like your efforts to explore careers or get better at resolving conflicts. Celebrate your public accomplishments, too—like Doing the Math and sharing your equation.

Cook (or bake) your favorite treats (recipes are equations, too!), gather your team, and enjoy being Ambassadors—together!

SAGE TEA, ANYONE?

Remember the recipe for Sage Tea that you learned early on in the journey? How about making some for this final celebration? Here are the directions:

Pour 1 cup of boiling water over 1 tablespoon of fresh sage leaves or 1–2 teaspoons of dried sage. Let steep for 3–5 minutes. Strain and add lemon and honey, if desired.

Sage Award Ceremony

This is one example of a ceremony Ambassadors might enjoy to celebrate the meaning of the Sage Award and all they have learned while earning it. The team can add to it, so that each girl has a chance to speak a line. Or they might add music or other creative touches, or invent a unique ceremony of their own for the occasion. What matters is that the girls take time to reflect on the wisdom they have gained along the journey, and maybe even their hopes for their next journey in Girl Scouts—or in life!

Ambassador 1: Sage comes from the Latin word *sapere*, to be wise.

Ambassador 2: Sage is also an herb, belonging to the botanical genus *Salvia*, from the Latin word *salvare*, meaning to heal or to save.

Ambassador 3 **(lights a candle and then speaks):** This light represents the justice we seek for Earth and all its inhabitants.

Ambassador 4: As a team and as individuals, we have tried to be sage—to find the wise decisions and healing efforts that create justice. We will each share a way in which we have:

- **Discovered** something new within ourselves—a value or quality that we can draw on as sages in search of justice.
- **Connected** with others to gain new perspectives.
- **Taken Action** toward making a lasting impact.

Allow quiet time for the girls to note their responses, perhaps in their book as a reminder of their journey. Then the Ambassadors share their reflections around the circle before continuing:

Ambassador 5: We will each present the Sage Award to a teammate and, in doing so, call out a quality she has that we admire and appreciate!

Ambassadors present the Sage Awards to one another.

Ambassador 6: In closing, let's remind ourselves of the full definition of environmental justice: "Environmental justice is the fair treatment and meaningful involvement of all people regardless of race, color, national origin, culture, education, or income with respect to the development, implementation, and enforcement of environmental laws, regulations, and policies."

Closing Circle (all Ambassadors): I will try to be sage in my life by . . .

P.S. Don't forget to blow out the candle!

Take Some Time for Yourself!

Now that the Ambassadors have started what may be a lifelong flight toward the ideal of justice, take a moment to nest a little.

In a quiet corner of your world, stop and congratulate yourself! You've guided Ambassadors to reach high, think hard, and have the courage to share a new vision. That's how change on Earth begins—with wise and healing leadership! Sages!

Not to mention that the girls have expanded their networks, explored careers, and maybe even resolved a conflict or two along the way.

Use the following reflection (similar to the one the girls have in the closing of their book) to think about all you have accomplished! Through your efforts with Ambassadors, how have you . . .

DISCOVERED something new within yourself—a value or quality that you use to inspire leadership in girls?

....

....

CONNECTED with others to gain new perspectives?

....

....

TAKEN ACTION toward making a lasting impact?

....

....

Now, go ahead, keep soaring. There's another Girl Scout adventure waiting for you, too!